Contents

Foreword

JOHN MONKS, General Secretary, TUC

When you read this publication, I hope you will take away three central messages.

The first, and most important, is that full employment is both desirable and achievable.

The second is that full employment is at the centre of the political debate, and must remain there.

The third is that the TUC means business in giving the trade union Movement an outward focus working with others on world of work issues.

The joint conference with the Employment Policy Institute was held to set a new agenda on full employment rolling.

This publication is not therefore simply a report of just another conference. I hope you will find it stimulating and a means to encourage further debate.

Above all, I hope you will want to join with the TUC, the Employment Policy Institute, and other organisations in taking that debate on. Our priority now is to move beyond the slogans and put flesh on the bones.

Many people – including the trade unions – will find this challenging. But a serious attempt to return to full employment must pose the difficult and awkward questions, and must develop the answers to them. I am confident that we can rise to that challenge.

JOHN MONKS
TUC General Secretary

Introduction

Anniversaries are often little more than an excuse for nostalgia. But every now and then an anniversary provides a valuable reference point for contemporary debate. This is undoubtedly true of this year's jubilee of two of the landmark publications of 1944: the wartime coalition's White Paper *Employment Policy* (cmnd 6527) and W. H. Beveridge's classic *Full Employment in a Free Society*.

The TUC, as part of its re-launch, decided to mark the fiftieth anniversary of these publications with a major conference – *Looking Forward to Full Employment* – that would build upon a renewed groundswell of interest in solutions to mass unemployment. At international level, 1994 has witnessed circulation of The European Commission's (Delors) White Paper on *Growth, Competitiveness and Employment,* the G7 industrial nations' wide-ranging 'Jobs Summit' held in Detroit, USA, and publication of the Organisation for Economic Co-operation and Development's detailed *Jobs Study.* At the same time, unemployment has climbed back toward the top of the domestic political agenda. Indeed, British politicians are once again beginning to talk the language of 'full employment'.

The Employment Policy Institute (EPI), an independent body, was invited to help to co-organise the conference. The aim was to ensure that the TUC was seen to be outward looking in its search for practical solutions and able to draw upon the best available research and current thinking on the jobs issue.

The conference – held at Congress House on July 5th – attracted a top level complement of speakers and delegates from politics, industry and academia, as well as from within the trade union movement (see Annex A). Most important of all, the conference offered a voice to unemployed people themselves. Delegates were provided with a set of specially commissioned background papers prepared by independent experts in the fields of economics, employment and public policy (see Annex B). A series of Action Profiles presented to the conference also outlined some practical ways in which social partnership is already helping to tackle unemployment (see Annex C).

The conference – which proved pivotal in the emerging jobs debate in Britain – spanned the entire range of issues that will need to be addressed if the rhetoric of full employment is to be turned into reality. This document contains a record of what was said by the main conference speakers and provides an overview of the issues raised in the background papers and discussion of them. But this document is not just a record. It also aims to set the agenda for full employment by considering some pointers for practical action, both immediate and long-term.

In Chapter 1, Rodney Bickerstaffe of UNISON (and a member of the TUC General Council) outlines why Britain needs to look forward to full employment by reference to the current scale of the unemployment problem. Unemployment is a major social as well as economic blight – as demonstrated by the human experiences contained in the chapter.

Chapter 2, by Andrew Britton, Director of the independent National Institute for Economic and Social Research, looks back to the post-war experience of full employment, asks whether full employment remains a realistic goal in a modern market economy, and considers the policy implications of a renewed commitment to full employment.

Chapter 3 contains the address to the conference by TUC General Secretary John Monks – which lays down the challenge of full employment in the 1990s – plus the response to that challenge from CBI Director General, Howard Davies and (the then) Employment Secretary, the Right Hon. David Hunt, MBE, MP. The views of Labour Party Employment Spokesperson, John Prescott, MP, and Alex Carlile, MP (then) Employment Spokesperson for the Liberal Democrats are presented in Chapter 4.

Chapter 5, by John Philpott, Director of the EPI, examines in a non-technical way some of the key analytical and related policy issues surrounding full employment. The Chapter incorporates points raised in the background papers prepared prior to the conference plus those made at the conference. By way of conclusion, Chapter 6 outlines a future agenda for practical action building upon the momentum set by the conference so that Britain really can begin to look forward to full employment.

CHAPTER 1

Mass unemployment – the scale of the problem

RODNEY BICKERSTAFFE, UNISON,
Member TUC General Council

Five Personal Experiences: **Mr Maurice Chittock,**
Mr Brian Rogers, Mr Tanveer Salam, Ms Angela Conlin
and Ms Maria Middleton

RODNEY BICKERSTAFFE, UNISON,
Member TUC General Council

Looking Forward to Full Employment is not just another conference. The event is a landmark and a turning point, both for the TUC and the wider debate on economic policy. For the TUC it is the first major conference with an explicit outward focus since our re-launch in March 1994. And the objective is quite clear – to put full employment at the top of the political agenda.

We should be in no doubt about the scale of the challenge (see Charts 1–4). Whether unemployment is three million, two million or one million, it is unacceptably high in a civilised society. And we know that there are at least two million other people who would like a job but are not unemployed by international criteria.

But the figure which should shame us all is the number of people out of work for more than a year – 1.2 million over the winter of 1993–94, more than four out of ten of all those unemployed. No answers to full employment will ever be convincing until they come up with ways of helping the long-term unemployed.

Nor can any answer be convincing until it addresses the needs of both men *and* women – and there are nearly one million women out of work in Britain today. We must also tackle the sheer waste of unemployment amongst our young people – nearly one in five of our under 20s are out of work. And we must confront the daily reality of discrimination against black workers in the labour market. Discrimination which leaves one in five black workers without a job, and many of those in work with only poor quality jobs.

These grim statistics come together in many of Britain's big cities – unemployment of 26 per cent in Hackney, 21 per cent in Manchester, 19 per cent in

Liverpool. The list could go on. It would seem incredible to a visitor from Mars that we could see such desperate and widespread unemployment side by side with so many unmet needs – the desperate state of the housing stock, the urgent need to improve our transport system and improve the environment. The TUC will soon be releasing a statement on public investment (see *Towards a Public Investment Strategy*, July 1994) as part of our campaign for full employment putting forward constructive and credible proposals for a targeted investment programme.

But the greatest single reason why unemployment must be our top priority for the 1990s is that unemployment creates and feeds off social ills that are tearing society and communities apart: poor health, both physical and mental; growing poverty; break-up of family life; social alienation; and attacks on racial and other minorities.

All these social problems are linked to unemployment, either directly or indirectly. Without a comprehensive solution to unemployment – such as a modern equivalent of that outlined in the 1944 White Paper *Employment Policy* – the social fabric will not survive intact.

I am not trying to be alarmist. This is a realistic prediction of what will happen if mass long-term unemployment persists at the levels we have seen over the past fifteen years.

The challenge for us all is to find an alternative way forward so that we can truly say that we are looking forward to full employment. And if we truly want to understand why we must do so we must first listen to the most important voice of all on this subject – a voice which is all too often ignored and patronised – that of the unemployed themselves. We therefore begin with the personal testimonies of Maurice Chittock, Brian Rogers, Tanveer Salam, Angela Conlin and Maria Middleton.

CHART 1: From White Paper to today – the unemployment record

1994 marks the 50th Anniversary of the White Paper *Employment Policy*. This set down the government's commitment to take responsibility for the level of employment in the economy.

Abandoned in 1979, this commitment has been replaced by a belief that unemployment can only be solved by individuals pricing themselves back into work. As the figure shows, this has not worked.

SUCCESS AND FAILURE – THE UNEMPLOYMENT RECORD OVER 40 YEARS

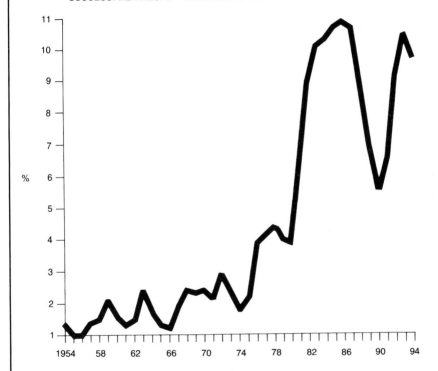

NOTE: Great Britain, Adjusted, First Quarter Average.

SOURCE: British Labour Statistics Historical Abstract: CSO Annual Supplement 1994; DE Gazette, April 1994.

9

CHART 2: World at work

But since the White Paper – and since 1979 – the world of work has changed radically. These changes create new opportunities and challenges. Some of them are set out below.

- in 1954 women made up just over one third of employees: in 1994 they account for almost a half;

- in the 1950s, less than one job in ten was part-time: in 1994 more than one job in four is part-time;

- in 1954 four workers out of ten worked in manufacturing: in 1994 less than two workers in ten work in this sector;

- in 1954 one worker in thirteen was self-employed; in 1994 one worker in eight is self-employed.

CHART 3: Unemployment in 1994

Official statistics using the International Labour Organisation (ILO) definition of unemployment show that one in ten people are out of work. They also show:

- nearly one million women are unemployed;

- one young person in five is out of work, double the national average;

- discrimination means more than one Black worker in five is unemployed;

- one man in eight is unemployed: other figures show one million claimants have been out of work for more than a year.

10

MAURICE CHITTOCK

My name is Maurice Chittock, from Northamptonshire. I do currently have a job, which I started in January this year – three years and one month after I was made redundant from my last full-time job. That had been my second experience of redundancy within six months from small firms of architects. It illustrates just a small part of the devastation of the construction industry which this recession has brought about.

After six months of unemployment, I reached the stage of doubting if I would ever have another full-time job. I feared that I could be facing a lifetime on the dole.

Three years at a school of architecture and eighteen years' experience designing and constructing buildings apparently counted for nothing. I was forced to abandon all of this, and look for other ways of trying to rebuild my working life.

But when I tried to find ways of gaining other training and qualifications, I found that the benefits system seemed to be specially designed to make this as difficult as possible. I could find no help and no way to start any full-time course. Consequently, I enrolled for a part-time degree course in computing. And now, three years later, I am just over half-way through it. But we have to pay all the course costs from my wife's earnings from teaching.

11

I now work as an Information Technology tutor, with unemployed people on "Training for Work" courses, for an organisation that relies on annual Training and Enterprise Council contracts. It is facing huge financial pressures. It means that come next April I could find myself back on the dole queue. But I earn less than two thirds of what I was getting in 1990 in actual money. All of this makes us very unsure of our future.

That sense of insecurity is something I know many others share. Almost everyone we know is still or has been out of work, feels that their job is threatened, or has a close relative unemployed. Neither do I see much to encourage me in the future, either for myself or my children. Economic boom and bust cycles, long-term mass unemployment – what sort of entry is that to the twenty-first century?

What sort of company would dare to keep ten or twenty per cent of its resources idle and wasted, while still claiming to be "efficient"? What morality is it that treats human beings as mere economic units, to be callously tossed aside at a moment's notice?

I see no reason at all to forgive those for whom *other* people's unemployment is "a price worth paying". I hope that this conference will begin to see those attitudes changed.

BRIAN ROGERS

I'm Brian Rogers from Nottingham. I'm 44 and have been unemployed for four years. The longest years of my life. Let me tell you how it happened to me. Eight years ago I accepted severance from British Coal after 20 years service. The country was coming out of recession. So I thought 'It's now or never'.

That was a fateful step. There were no jobs. So I joined Employment Training (ET) and did three months as a pipe fitter. Only to find myself jobless at the end.

Then I got a job as a security guard working 90 hours for a pittance of £160 a week. They did not bother to renew my contract. So back to ET again and then of course the dole. I soon found that ET is a revolving door leading to the dole queue.

Then last February the final blow. The knock on the door. The eviction order. The mortgage company demanded that I pay the arrears at £700 a month. How could someone on £66.60 a week pay that? Even if I paid all my income support to the building society I couldn't have paid half their demand. So we lost our house. But not our dignity.

Now I'm on another scheme. It's called Training for Work. I'm training to do maintenance work in a hotel – for my dole and a tenner. Let's hope it will really lead to work this time.

That's my story. But it's no different from many stories. What I am concerned about is the scale and pace of future job losses.

As a former British Coal worker I am appalled at this Government closing most of our pits. I was born and bred in the Northumberland coalfield. There is now not one pit open in the North East.

Fifty eight years ago 200 Jarrow marchers petitioned Parliament to recognise their right to work. That's what we've got to demand today.

We must demand that the Government stop privatising and begin investing. Investing in training. Investing in jobs. Investing in our future. But most of all investing in Britain.

Tell them we want jobs not excuses. The right to work. Real work with proper pay. Not working for our dole. That's how we can put the 'Great' back into Britain.

TANVEER SALAM

My name is Tanveer Salam. I live in Luton with my wife and three children. I've been unemployed now for two and a half years.

I came to this country at sixteen. Full of hope. I went to college to study radio and TV electronics. And I obtained my City and Guilds Part One certificate. My aim was to enter an electronics apprenticeship to increase my skills. But no employer would take me on. I was *too* old. I was *nineteen*.

So I joined London Underground. I did well. Rising to senior craftsman and even a craft examiner. But then disaster struck. I suffered an industrial injury in the workshop. As a result I lost my job. The small industrial injuries compensation I received cannot compensate for my lost earnings. I'm now bringing up my family on income support.

I've done what the government has told us unemployed to do. Joined a Job Club. Entered a Job Interview Guarantee (JiG) Scheme. I've applied for over sixty jobs this year and had only one interview. Most of the companies didn't even bother to reply.

The Luton Unemployed centre has however helped me a great deal. I now know that unemployment is not just a personal problem for families. It can blight whole communities. It is the breeding ground for racial hatred, as we have seen in Tower Hamlets.

What really worries me is the fact that so many young people today are without work, without hope. I want them to have the apprenticeships – the chances – that I never had. The future of our country lies in the skills of our young people. They deserve nothing less.

Ms ANGELA CONLIN

My name is Angela Conlin, I am a volunteer welfare advisor at Clydebank Unemployed Centre. My husband who has been unemployed for the past six months, is also a member of the centre.

On leaving school in 1984 with various 'O' levels I decided that rather than take on a Youth Training Scheme I would obtain a full-time position in the hotel industry. This ultimately led on to various unskilled, low paid jobs.

The abolition of the Wages Council in 1993 has further eroded the wage rates of the type of work that I had been previously employed in. I have two young children. Childcare is not in any real sense readily available in Scotland. Any childcare on offer when employed has to be paid for. Low paid workers earn *less* than the charges for quality childcare.

In 1991 it became increasingly obvious that I would have to retrain and seek further education to expand my employment opportunities. Between 1991 and 1994 I achieved several new qualifications. I enrolled at college and succeeded in earning an SVQ II and gaining 10 Scotvec modules. I also gained Scotvec modules in Word Processing and Spreadsheets in the Unemployed Centre.

The good news is that I have been able to put to good use some of the experiences gained. My voluntary work at the centre has enhanced my previous qualifications and restored my self confidence. In the meantime my skills are helping other members of the community, in particular the unemployed and individuals with disabilities.

My voluntary work would not be possible if creche facilities were not provided free of charge at the centre. It offers creche facilities for all areas of participation – education, leisure and voluntary work.

I have mentioned my drive to further retrain and further educate myself. I now look forward to favourable employment. I'm not unemployed through choice. *I want to work*. Unemployment represents a desperate economic waste of skill, talents, abilities and resources.

Ms MARIA MIDDLETON

I'm Maria Middleton from Wakefield. It is a privilege to represent unemployed people at this conference and in particular the Wakefield TUC Centre for the Unemployed.

I've been unemployed for three years now. When my son married I thought it would be the ideal time to get a full-time job. But once you reach the wrong side of forty no prospect of work exists. No employers want to know. You have no chance of proving your worth. You are one of the forgotten people.

All we want is to take more control over our lives again. I believe that full employment *can* be achieved. And this conference is proof of that.

We unemployed are not on our knees. The TUC unemployment centres see to that. They provide a lifeline of friendship, support, and stimulation for unemployed people like myself. Our centres bind people together in a great community spirit in areas such as Yorkshire blighted by unemployment.

The Centre's work is helped by trade unions. The one-fund-for-all-OFFA scheme ensures that working trade unionists can contribute financially to help the centres. A shining example of the way employed people can help the unemployed.

The Government continually harass us on to their schemes. We are put on a merry-go-round. Changing from one scheme to another with no job in sight.

I, like many other unemployed people, have decided to make a fresh start. Two years ago I enrolled on a part-time course and have completed my Certificate of Higher Education. Now I am planning to go on for the degree.

We, the unemployed, have a right to expect jobs in the future. We have the right to make a real contribution to the nation and the right to a fair share of its wealth. This conference is an important step towards achieving this.

CHAPTER 2

Full employment in a market economy

ANDREW BRITTON, Director,
National Institute for Economic and Social Research

Introduction

The occasion for this conference is the 50th anniversary of the White Paper on *Employment Policy*, Cmnd 6527, presented by the Minister of Reconstruction to Parliament in May 1944. It is a short paper, just 31 pages long, and much of that length is devoted to the special difficulties in the labour market that were expected during the transition from War to Peace. The detailed policy proposals set out in the White Paper were not implemented in quite the way that was foreseen. Nevertheless this slim document did signal a new approach to economic policy quite different to the approach of governments pre-war. The most important sentence is the first: 'The Government accept as one of their primary aims and responsibilities the maintenance of a high and stable level of employment after the war'. The paper would have been a landmark in the history of economic policy if it had said no more than that.

To understand the significance of the commitment contained in the White Paper, we should turn to a very influential book, also published in 1944: *Full Employment in a Free Society* by William Beveridge. There we can find the reason for the commitment being made and also a fuller account of the methods by which it was hoped that full employment would be maintained. That will be my starting point for an overview of the successes and failures of economic policy, then and now. Why was full employment adopted as an objective of policy? Why was it achieved and maintained so successfully for more than twenty years after the White Paper was published? Why has it not been maintained since the 1970s? Should the commitment to full employment be reiterated today? What does it mean in today's circumstances? And, since there is no point in making commitments which cannot be fulfilled, what policy actions should follow.

I have called my paper (and this chapter) 'Full employment in a market economy' to emphasise the difference between the circumstances of today and those in which Beveridge wrote fifty years ago. Whether we welcome the fact or not, the organisation of economic life is very different now from that of the post-war years. There is no question of turning back the clock. If there is something in the commitment to full employment which still seems right, even compelling, in 1994, then we need to face some hard and difficult choices if we are to convince a contemporary audience that this is more than a political slogan.

Post-war consensus

The long periods of high unemployment between the wars had been the cause of poverty of a kind we no longer know in this country. The unemployed and their families had experienced severe hardship, even hunger. One of the main concerns of Beveridge and of the wartime coalition Government was that a social security system should be established which would prevent this happening again. Such provision, it was recognised, would be difficult to finance unless the level of unemployment was kept low. But that was not the main reason for making the commitment to full employment.

To quote Beveridge: "Idleness is not the same as want, but a separate evil, which men do not escape by having an income. They must also have the chance of rendering useful service and of feeling that they are doing so". He also wrote "A person who has difficulty in buying the labour that he wants suffers inconvenience or reduction of profits. A person who cannot sell his labour is in effect told that he is of no use. The first difficulty causes annoyance or loss. The other is a personal catastrophe".

He gave three further reasons why full employment should be maintained: to prevent the growth of restrictive practices; to make structural change in the economy more acceptable; and to provide a stimulus to technical progress and the more productive use of labour. No doubt behind this lay also a profound unease as to the political implications of high unemployment. On the title page of his book Beveridge put the quotation 'misery generates hate'. That had indeed been the experience of the inter-war years. The rise of the dictatorships owed much to the perceived failure of liberal democracies to provide prosperity and jobs. It had to be demonstrated that a free society was capable of delivering full employment. The alternative to a free society was to imitate either Nazi Germany or Soviet Russia. The political consensus over economic policy after the war rested on the belief that full employment was essential to the survival of the freedoms that were believed to be fundamental by all the major political parties, and which the war had been fought to preserve.

The importance of war-time experience should never be underestimated as an explanation of post-war economic policies. In war, of course, full employment had been achieved. Useful work was found for everyone as part of a national effort, even those who had been thought unemployable turned out to be good soldiers or munitions workers after all. It could all be put down to good planning and a general willingness to co-operate. Workers and management found themselves, most of the time at least, on the same side. Much of economic life was regulated in the interests of the war effort, and despite some absurdities, regulation seemed to work well. The stimulus for efficiency or initiative came mainly from the need to serve a common purpose. Those who made profits for themselves were regarded as selfish and anti-social. The sense of a common purpose remained after the war was won and helped to support the continued existence of regulations and restrictions on economic life which might otherwise have been found to be intolerable.

Beveridge was well aware of the need for voluntary co-operation if full employment was to be made compatible with economic freedom. He wrote: 'The degree of liberty . . . which can be left to agencies independent of the State, without imperilling the policy of full employment, depends on the responsibility and public spirit with which those liberties are exercised. There is no reason to doubt that the responsibility and public spirit will be forthcoming'.

But the main requirement for full employment, according to the White Paper or to Beveridge, was neither regulation nor public spirit; these on their own would not be sufficient. What was essential, according to the post-war intellectual consensus, was an adequate level of aggregate demand. The diagnosis put forward by Maynard Keynes of the cause of unemployment between the wars led to an obvious prescription. The second paragraph of the White Paper begins thus: 'A country will not suffer from mass unemployment so long as the total demand for its goods and services is maintained at a high level'. The implications of this are set out later in the Paper: 'The Government are prepared to accept in future the responsibility for taking action at the earliest possible stage to avert a threatened slump. This involves a new approach and a new responsibility for the State'.

The new approach is well described by Beveridge as the creation of a 'seller's market' for labour. He defined full employment as being a state in which there were 'more vacant jobs than unemployed men'. Moreover these should be 'Jobs at fair wages of such a kind, and so located that the unemployed men can reasonably be expected to take them'. It is important to recognise that this is what full employment meant for Beveridge: not a state of balance or equilibrium in the labour market, but rather a state of labour scarcity, so that anyone who wanted work would not have to look for long to find it. Of course he realised the danger of inflation in such a situation, but he relied on the public spirit and responsibility of employers and especially trade unions to keep this tendency in check.

The main instruments for securing an adequate level of demand were, according to Beveridge, to be extra public spending, both current and capital, and the regulation of private investment by a National Investment Board. He criticised the White Paper as too timid, in its reluctance to intervene in the private sector and for its continuing concern with the sale of public sector debt. Very little was said either by Beveridge or in the White Paper about monetary policy. It was widely believed at the same time that the rate of interest had little effect on saving or investment. Hence it was on fiscal policy that the architects of full employment relied for the management of aggregate demand.

Demand management was the main post-war policy innovation that supported the commitment to full employment, but it was not the only one. The White Paper also discussed regional or local unemployment and proposed to tackle it in three ways: by encouraging firms to locate in 'development areas'; by removing obstacles to labour mobility; and by providing facilities for training.

Looking back 50 years later we cannot but admire the courage with which the commitment to full employment was made. It was by no means clear at the time that the objective could be achieved. Indeed, all recent history suggested that it could not. In fact the White Paper was quite cautious in its wording, speaking of 'a high and stable level of employment' rather than the more emotive words used by Beveridge. And Beveridge himself thought that a reasonable target to aim at would be three per cent unemployment, or 550 thousand. 'This margin would consist of a shifting body of short-term unemployed who could be maintained without hardship by unemployment insurance'. In fact unemployment was below that level throughout the 1950s and for most of the 1960s as well.

The years of full employment

In 1964, twenty years after the White Paper was issued, the National Institute published an historical study *The Management of the British Economy, 1945–60* by Christopher Dow. In his conclusions he wrote: 'In terms of its fundamental aim – the desire so to manage the economy as to prevent the heavy unemployment that accompanied the pre-war trade cycle – modern economic policy has clearly been a success. For some years after the war, high unemployment required no specific intervention: wartime arrears of demand were more than enough to ensure full employment. In the decade of the fifties, however, there probably would have been more unemployment if the Government had not intervened to increase demand when unemployment showed signs of increasing: and, perhaps equally important, if the world of business had not acquired some confidence that governments could and would so intervene when necessary'. He then goes on to point out other economic problems, such as low but persistent inflation, frequent balance-of-payments weakness, and growth rather slower than in many other countries. But he adds: 'Failure in these respects has been relative failure only'. At that stage the main emphasis was, quite rightly, on what went right, and not on the early signs of what would later go sadly wrong.

We cannot be certain even now why it was that demand remained so strong for many years after the war. It was not because the Government, following the teachings of Keynes and Beveridge, borrowed heavily to finance extra spending. They did not need to, because private expenditure was buoyant most of the time. Initially private sector demand may have been strengthened by the low level of interest rates and by the devaluation of sterling in 1949. But this is not enough to explain the continuing buoyancy of expenditure well into the 1960s, by which time the authorities were more inclined to rein it back than to urge it forward.

We are concerned here with a phenomenon which affected most advanced industrial countries, not just the United Kingdom. Initially it may be attributed to making good the damage done by the war to buildings and equipment both in the public and private sectors. The Cold War and the Korean War stimulated military spending. Consumers for many years were running down the savings accumulated during the years of rationing, then borrowing to acquire new durable goods as they became available. The expansion of international trade was catching up with opportunities lost, not only in wartime but also as a result of trade restrictions in the 1930s.

The point I would wish to stress however is that demand and supply were not matched exactly together by some extraordinary skill on the part of policy-makers, nor indeed by any flexibility in the workings of the market mechanism. What seems to have characterised the period rather was a condition of persistently high, and at times excess, demand. We did have, as Beveridge intended, a 'seller's market' for labour.

It becomes important therefore to ask what were the restraints which prevented wages and prices rising to remove the excess demand, as would be expected in a market economy. Part of the answer may be with the size of the public sector, as well as the continued regulation of credit, foreign exchange, and investment. But I am also prepared to recognise the importance of what Beveridge called 'responsibility and public spirit' as a restraint on inflationary pressure. There was a very general agreement on the priority to be given to full employment, and memories of the inter-war years were still fresh. In national wage bargaining there was some recognition of the potential conflict between the national aims of full employment and price stability. Perhaps the trade unions did not at first realise the strength of their bargaining position in a 'seller's market' for labour, or they chose not to use that strength. Either way, they were contributing to the persistence of what now appears to us as a golden age. By the mid 1960s it was already becoming clear that the problems with inflation, the balance of payments and international competitiveness were getting progressively more serious. Since the early 1970s the commitment to 'a high and stable level of employment', although never formally abandoned, has never actually been fulfilled.

What went wrong?

I hardly need to rehearse again the history of unemployment in this country since 1970. The trend has been strongly upward, at least until the mid-1980s. The fluctuations from year to year have also become much more severe. For much of the time inflation has been very high and very variable, although it is low and stable now. The experience of other countries has been varied, but also generally unhappy. In most European countries the trend of unemployment has been strongly upward; in the United States the level has generally been high although the increase is not so marked. There is no consensus amongst economists about the explanation of these developments; on the contrary the period has been one of confusion, controversy and disarray.

It is helpful to distinguish between cyclical and structural unemployment. There is plenty of evidence that the pressure of demand rises and falls from year to year and that unemployment moves in sympathy with that cycle. For example, unemployment fell sharply following the boom in the late 1980s, rose again during the recession of the early 1990s, and is now falling again. This cyclical movement does seem to be related to the adequacy of demand in the economy as a whole, in much the way that Keynes described. However, this cyclical movement, troublesome though it may be, is not the main issue. The main issue is the high level around which the fluctuation occurs, and the dramatic increase in the average level of unemployment in the 1970s and 1980s.

It is difficult to argue that this increase was attributable in any simple way to a deficiency of aggregate demand, since it was not matched by other indications of increasing spare capacity and since it was accompanied by bursts of rapid inflation. We must therefore address the problem of 'structural unemployment', or an increase in the NAIRU (the level of unemployment at which inflation is held constant) or an increase in the equilibrium or 'natural' rate of unemployment. But attaching labels to unemployment tells us little or nothing about its origin, or its remedy. I shall summarise the possible explanations of structural unemployment under three headings: hysteresis, sclerosis and skedasticity. If these sound like the names of serious diseases, that is appropriate enough, because they all represent something going seriously wrong with the workings of the economy.

Hysteresis in this context means the long-lasting, perhaps even the permanent, effect of an accident or stress to the system. Thus the shocks caused by the two increases in world oil prices during the 1970s each produced a sharp contraction of activity in most countries, including the United Kingdom, cyclical downturns much larger than those of the 1950s and 1960s. The hysteresis theories turn on the idea that the associated sharp rises in unemployment were difficult even impossible to reverse. For example the investment, the training and even the technical improvements which should have taken place during the years of recession may not have been made good, even when growth was resumed. Another theory of the same kind suggests that the workers made redundant in a recession lose contact with the labour market, are no longer protected by their union, are regarded with suspicion by employers and become demoralised or demotivated. If this kind of theory is correct we do not need a different theory for the trend from that of the cycle. A succession of severe cycles would be enough to explain the whole story. My own view is that this explanation, although it is important, is not enough to account for all of the upward trend.

Sclerosis, blames the rise in unemployment on a lack of flexibility. It is the main explanation given in the recent *Jobs Study* published by the OECD, and in the Mais lecture by the Chancellor of the Exchequer this year. According to this view the difficulty is one of matching demand and supply for labour. Relative wages do not change quickly enough to clear the market, if indeed they move at all. Workers are reluctant to change their location or occupation, or to learn new skills. According to this view there does exist a labour market equilibrium at which full employment would be restored, but the market takes a very long time indeed to reach it, especially in Europe.

Those who favour sclerosis theories would claim that the problem has got much worse since the 1960s. The need for adjustment has become greater, but the ability to adjust has become less. They point to rigidities introduced into labour markets, especially in Europe, in the 1960s and 1970s. These include increased union power, increased regulation of terms and conditions of employment, greater job security (which could ironically increase unemployment by making firms reluctant to take on new staff) and the statutory enforcement of minimum wages. The weakness of the theory is that the economy was highly regulated, and in a sense inflexible, during the war and for some time afterwards; yet then we had full employment. I am in favour of flexibility, of course, but I am not convinced that an increase in inflexibility can explain the rise in unemployment since the 1960s, at least so far as the UK is concerned.

Skedasticity is a term I have invented to describe those theories which emphasise the variation or inequality of earning power in the labour force. Suppose that this inequality has increased for some reason, but that the inequality of actual wages cannot increase, because of minimum wage provisions or the level of unemployment benefits. The result will be higher unemployment. The possible reasons for a widening in the dispersion of earning power are many and various. Some blame international trade, especially imports from low-wage countries; some blame new technology, which benefits the average worker but not the least skilled; some blame the increased participation of women especially in relatively low-paid jobs, others blame an actual deterioration in training and education. The situation could be made worse by increased competition between firms obliging them to eliminate any job which is not essential, and to make quite sure that none of their employees are paid any more than a strict assessment of their contribution to the business would justify.

I should emphasise that these theories do *not* suggest that trade, technology, competition and so on are bad for the economy as a whole. On the contrary, the point is that they *do* raise average living standards and average pay, but this means that the minimum level of pay which employers will offer or workers will accept also goes up – and that leaves a significant minority with no work at all. I suspect that theories which emphasise the problems of inequality and low skills do explain a good deal of the increase in unemployment, particularly in the UK.

So we do not lack explanations of the rise in unemployment, nor suggestions for policies to reverse it. As inflation and unemployment rose from the mid-1960s to the late 1970s the initial response of policy was to try to repair the post-war consensus. By this stage it was evident that the problems of rising prices and balance of payments deficits were so serious that the Government could not restore full employment simply by adding to demand. For the twenty years or so after the war it was possible to maintain a 'seller's market' for labour, as Beveridge had wished. But this could continue only so long as a combination of regulation and co-operation kept the lid on price and wage inflation. The lid was blown off in the 1970s and no attempt to put it back on again has succeeded for long. We have had to reduce the temperature, that is to say the pressure of demand in the economy. A market economy cannot operate with a persistent excess of demand.

A great deal has changed in the labour market since we last experienced full employment. New developments of technology, especially information technology, have transformed working conditions requiring new skills and making old skills obsolete. The participation of women has increased and with that has grown the practice of part-time working. Self-employment has become much more widespread. Job changes have become more frequent, and employment has become less secure. The influence of trade unions in wage bargaining has declined, although they still have an important role to play and still have popular support. Management has become more scientific (at least the jargon it uses sounds more scientific) and its approach to employment has become more businesslike – perhaps because competition between firms has become more intense. To sum up, we have seen the evolution of a market economy in this country, much more like the market described in economic textbooks, and it is in that context that the issue of full employment must now be addressed.

What does full employment mean now?

Since Beveridge wrote about full employment much has changed, but much also remains the same. It is still true that enforced idleness destroys self-respect and that 'misery generates hate'. There is still the same need to belong to society, to serve and to be valued. For most people, indeed for more of the population than in earlier generations, this need to belong can be satisfied only by participation in the economy, in paid work, part-time or full-time, permanent or temporary, for an employer or for your own business. High levels of unemployment have not destroyed liberal democracy as seemed possible in the 1940s, but they have divided society and alienated a substantial minority. We have to ask what kind of society we want to live in. I think that most people would say that they want a society in which everyone is able to participate, in which there is effective access for all to work in exchange for an income. The work is important as well as the income because it is still true, as Beveridge said, that idleness is a separate evil from want and that no-one should be told by society that they have nothing useful to contribute.

Looking into the far distant future we can perhaps imagine a world in which the need for work has been almost eliminated, a world in which the machines have taken over most of the jobs now done by human hands or brains. In such a world if it ever exists, and I am not sure it will, most of the population would in a sense be idle most of the time. But it would be idleness of a very different kind from that now experienced by the unemployed. It would be a voluntary idleness, a life of leisure chosen in preference to work, or indeed a life of voluntary work undertaken for its own sake and with no financial reward. Because it would affect the workforce as a whole it would not be socially divisive. It may be useful to speculate about such possibilities and to consider their implications for society, sometime in the twenty-first century. But this does not help us to solve the urgent problem of involuntary unemployment today and the need for all who wish to participate in economic life to be given an opportunity to do so.

We cannot be certain that this need to participate will necessarily be satisfied in a market economy. In the property market buildings can stand empty for years; in the market for consumer goods some of the stock has to be written off. If we treat labour as simply another commodity to be bought and sold, then it is human lives that will sometimes be written off and declared to be redundant. It is appropriate to use emotive language, because the issue here is one of feelings rather than calculation. We want the labour market to be humane in its treatment of individuals, as well as efficient, and we may fear that it is becoming less so. This is in part a matter of the way in which employers and employees choose to behave towards one another, but it is a matter of public policy as well.

For many professional economists unemployment is the most important policy issue of all. We see our role as contributing to the solution of a social problem, not just making the economy more productive. We would be most reluctant to abandon the objective of full employment, because it points beyond economics to a goal which is not just increasing individual utility but also the cohesion of society as a whole.

Setting full employment as a policy objective, even in the context of a market economy, makes it clear that society as a whole has an interest in the way that individuals are treated. It does involve the concept of a community and something which Beveridge called 'public spirit'. We need, in the very different circumstances of today, to find the institutional setting within which that common purpose can be achieved.

Clearly there is no way in which society can underwrite the continued existence of particular jobs or even occupations. Neither can there be a right to a job of one's own choosing at a wage one considers fair. A commitment to full employment will leave many individual ambitions unsatisfied and hopes disappointed. There will still be closures and redundancies, but perhaps we can find a better way of dealing with the consequences. Perhaps we can prevent people being too dependent on the continuation of a particular job and widen the opportunities they have to recover from misfortune when it hits them.

If this is to be achieved then in practice something may well have to be given up in return. The recipe for full employment proposed by Keynes was in effect a 'free lunch'. By making good the deficiency in demand everyone could be better off. If, however, unemployment is now a structural problem then it is unlikely that a painless cure can be found for it. One interpretation of the rise in unemployment is that society has given up the aim of full employment because it found the cost in terms of other objectives was too great. Perhaps no such conscious choice was ever actually made. If, however, we are now to make the deliberate choice that full employment is to be given priority then we need to know what else is being given up. To make a choice between aims we need to know the means that will be adopted. I turn therefore to the question of how a commitment to full employment in a market economy might actually be fulfilled.

There is no shortage of recent studies of unemployment, certainly no shortage of policy recommendations. In the past two years extensive work has been done on the subject both by the European Commission and by the OECD. The latter organisation has produced not one solution to the problem but sixty. It may be inevitable that international organisations, which have to take account of the very different situations in all their member states, will produce recommendations with no clear single focus. Moreover there is a natural tendency, not confined to international organisations, to include within the policy menu a large number of reforms which could be thought worthwhile in their own right but which are at best of marginal value in relation to unemployment. Those who favour causes as diverse as privatisation, European integration, or nursery education will want to argue that they have found something to offer as part of the package. Those who are looking around for attractive ingredients to put in the package will find these offers difficult to resist. But if we are serious about achieving full employment then we must concentrate on the search for policies which will really make a big difference.

Macroeconomic policy

It follows from what I have already written that the problem of unemployment cannot be solved by macroeconomic policy on its own, simply by more public spending, by tax cuts or lower interest rates. We have quite recent evidence of the effects of stimulating aggregate demand. In the late 1980s, partly as a result of credit liberalisation, partly as a result of tax cuts, both consumer spending and fixed investment accelerated. The result for a few years was a rapid growth of output. In some parts of the country at least there was briefly a 'seller's market' for many kinds of labour, as national unemployment fell sharply and skill shortages developed. But the consequences were rapid growth of imports, renewed inflation and an increase in interest rates. The expansion had to be stopped and there followed one of the most severe recessions since the war.

We are now in the recovery phase of the cycle, with unemployment falling again and capacity utilisation rising. Macroeconomic policy became expansionary after sterling was forced out of the Exchange Rate Mechanism, and the

26

impetus given by the depreciation and reduction in interest rates is still carrying the economy forward despite the tax increases coming into effect this year. There is some purely cyclical fall in unemployment still to come, but on the basis of past experience I do not think that the level can be held much below two to two-and-a-half millions. Several years of really rapid growth of output, unless it was accompanied by improved competitiveness and growth of capacity, would lead only to fresh problems of inflation and for the balance of payments. There are some optimists who believe that the level of structural unemployment, the NAIRU or the equilibrium rate (whatever term one uses) is already much lower than that, perhaps no more than one million, thanks to the free market policies introduced since 1979. There is not much evidence from the behaviour of the aggregate economy to support that view. I would like to believe it is true, but I shall proceed on the assumption that it is not.

If structural unemployment is indeed of the order of two to two-and-a-half millions then there is not much more that can be achieved by demand expansion. The management of demand does, nevertheless, still have an important part to play in a strategy to achieve full employment. As has already been indicated, one theory of structural unemployment sees it as a legacy of past recessions. If it were possible to keep the economy growing steadily, with no recessions, and no unsustainable booms either, then it is more likely that the damage done by the instability of the last twenty years can gradually be put right.

A great deal has been learnt about the management of demand since the White Paper was issued fifty years ago. Far more statistical information is available and econometric models have been developed to improve forecasting methods. Nevertheless, the record of demand management has been disappointing. We know, from many years of experience, the inevitable limitations of economic forecasting, and hence the difficulty of taking timely action to offset the economic cycle. The White Paper said in 1944 that 'the Government are prepared to accept in the future the responsibility for taking action at the earliest possible stage to avert a threatened slump'. I think the Government is still prepared to play that role if it can, and that a long-drawn out slump could probably be corrected, but clearly it is not always possible to avert a sharp recession.

Given the limits of demand management it would be very beneficial if more stability could be built into the economic system itself. A relatively free market economy may be more prone to cyclical variation than the more regulated economy of the post-war period. The British economy seems to have had a more bumpy ride than most other economies in Europe. Possible reasons for this include the structure of financial markets and the importance of homeownership. These considerations are relevant to the problem of unemployment, and need to be considered in that context, but obviously more direct action is needed as well, if a commitment to full employment is to be fulfilled.

Industrial policy and international competitiveness

The foreword to the 1944 White Paper ends with the following sentence: 'But the success of the policy outlined in this Paper will ultimately depend on the understanding and support of the community as a whole – and especially on the efforts of employers and workers in industry; for without a rising standard of industrial efficiency we cannot achieve a high level of employment combined with a rising standard of living'. The point is an important one and still valid today.

There are those who believe that the whole economy needs to be strengthened and reformed before full employment can be achieved. They stress the need for greater industrial efficiency and competitiveness if Britain is to participate in the open markets of Europe and the world as a whole. This broad approach is particularly attractive if it could make possible an increase in industrial employment at the same time as real wages were rising. Moreover the potential constraint on growth arising from the deficit on the balance of payments would be lifted if Britain's trade performance were improved.

The White Paper published by the European Commission last December puts great emphasis on improved industrial competitiveness as the best approach to job creation. Implicitly it is assuming that Europe can gain employment at the expense of other industrial countries for example America and Japan. (The OECD *Jobs Study* report prepared for the governments of all industrial countries jointly on the other hand could not make recommendations which would help some member states at the expense of others.) In considering policy options for the UK we must remember that considerable scope remains for raising our standards of performance and productivity to match those of our continental neighbours. Indeed a considerable effort may be needed to ensure that we do not fall further behind.

Having accepted all this, it would nevertheless be wrong to concentrate too much attention in this paper on industrial policy. In the first place there is no agreement as to the actual policy measures which are most likely to achieve the desired result of improving Britain's competitivenes and efficiency. Whilst some economists argue for a 'developmental' approach, which would involve some kind of national planning, others regard that with disdain and see the proper role of the state as confined to regulation – and no more of that than is unavoidable. I do not need to take sides in that debate on this occasion.

The second reason for placing the main emphasis elsewhere is real doubt as to the scale of effects of unemployment which could be achieved by industrial policy of any kind. One could imagine a successful industrial policy which achieved its main goal of improving international competitiveness, whilst leaving the problem of structural unemployment largely unsolved. The theories of what I have called 'skedasticity' attribute unemployment to the distribution within the workforce of skills and other characteristics relevant to employment. If this approach is right we need to concentrate on the lower end of that distribution, not on the midpoint. It is to policies with that focus that I turn next.

Labour market policies

We now have a great deal of experience of special employment measures in this country, and plenty of examples to draw on from the experience of other countries as well if we wish. The list of schemes gets longer and longer, although many of the new ones turn out to be variations on themes which have been tried out before. There have been selective employment subsidies and schemes to promote employment in the public sector. More recently the emphasis has been more on help with searching for work and tightening up the conditions for the receipt of benefit. At the most, these schemes may have reduced unemployment by a few hundred thousand each year since the mid-1970s.

Proposals to introduce similar schemes on a much larger scale run into problems of administrative feasibility. If unemployment was low, say half-a-million or a million in total, then it would be possible to consider each case individually, and to show a genuine care on behalf of society. Training and counselling could be provided on a generous scale. Every effort could be made to find or to create jobs which are within the capability of each unemployed person. It might even be right, in that context, to insist that job offers are not refused. One could readily imagine an employment 'fallback' provision, even an employment guarantee of some kind to cope with a relatively small number of people who for one reason or another have difficulty in finding or keeping employment. But I do not think that mass unemployment, running to two millions or more, can be tackled in this way. The task becomes unmanageable and the expense becomes prohibitive.

It might be possible by something akin to conscription to create work of a kind for even two million unemployed, but there would be no question of giving individual attention to the needs or the potential abilities of such vast numbers. It would mean creating a large regimented sector clearly differentiated from the rest of the economy. This is not at all what Beveridge had in mind when he wrote about full employment. The underlying purpose of renewing that commitment today could not be fulfilled by special employment measures on a gigantic scale. The social marginalisation and alienation caused by unemployment would remain, and the need to feel that everyone belongs to the community would not be satisfied. On a small scale they undoubtedly have an important part to play, and it matters a great deal how that role is performed. But they cannot be the main means by which a promise to restore full employment would be kept.

Taxes and subsidies

In a market economy economic policy works best by influencing relative costs and prices, by creating incentives for individuals or firms to behave in a socially-desired way. Thus the burning of fuel which may threaten the environment is not prohibited or rationed, but it is taxed. Energy saving is not made compulsory, but it is encouraged by subsidies. A similar approach could work in the labour market.

The aim is not to encourage employment as such, but to increase the employment opportunities for those who, for any reason, are likely to earn wages well below the average. This relates to the dispersion or skedasticity theory of unemployment. We want to offset the widening in the range of earning power which seems to be one reason for the upward trend in unemployment. The Chancellor took a small step in that direction last November when he reduced by one per cent the National Insurance (NI) contributions of lower paid employees and widened the 20p income tax band. Could the same approach, on a very much larger scale, be the centre-piece of a strategy to restore full employment?

Taxes and subsidies apply to the population as a whole, not just to particular individuals identified as requiring individual attention. The state operates at arms length. No-one has to be identified as requiring special help; there is no need to interfere in their lives or question their motivation. Unlike special employment measures, taxes and benefits can operate on a very large scale without the danger of stigma or marginalisation.

If the intention is to encourage employment creation then the natural place to start reform is with national insurance contributions, as the Chancellor has already indicated. I shall not attempt to go into any detail, but two general points can be made. The first is that employees' contributions must in the long run influence employment prospects just as much as do employers' contributions. The need is to improve incentives to seek employment as well as incentives to provide it. If the employers' contribution is cut then there will be a tendency for wages to rise because the demand for labour will increase, and if the employees' contribution is cut there will be a tendency for wages to fall because the supply of labour will increase. The net effect on labour costs and take-home pay should be much the same in the end – and the graduation of contributions should relate to pay per hour. The intention is to improve the employment prospects for those most at risk of unemployment, that is those whose earning power is relatively low, whether they work full-time or part-time.

Whilst national insurance contributions are the natural place to start, the reforms could affect other forms of taxation as well. Income tax thresholds could be raised. But if the wish is to focus specifically on earned income then there would need to be a new form of tax allowance designed with that in mind. This too would need to be related to pay per hour – an innovation so far as the tax system is concerned.

Instead of cutting national insurance contributions a very similar result could be achieved by subsidies to employers, also related to pay per hour. For the lowest paid it might be necessary for the subsidy to represent a large proportion of the wage before sufficient growth of employment could be induced.

One of the merits of a general tax cut or employment subsidy for the low paid is that we do not have to know in advance where the new jobs will be created. That can be left to the market to decide, so long as the state does not stand in the way. My own guess is that many of them would be in services, and more generally in sectors which do not compete with imports. This inevitably points to activities, for example health and education, which are largely in the public sector. If this approach is to be effective, then employment by central and local government must be allowed to increase even if total public spending is left unchanged. It would be absurd to adopt a target of full employment and then say that the public sector is not allowed to contribute to its achievement.

If the problem of employment is addressed in this way it is bound to be expensive in terms of revenue; there can be no disguising that. Large sums of money must be involved if a large effect is to be achieved. If the reform succeeded in its aim of reducing unemployment permanently to a tolerable level then there would be substantial savings on benefits now paid to those out of work. That would be an important offset to the gross cost of the reform to the exchequer. Nevertheless I suspect that the net cost would still be large. The political process must indicate whether society is prepared to pay that cost, and if so in what form the revenue should be raised. Options worth considering would include higher NI contributions from the better paid, higher rates of VAT or taxes on energy. None of these would be popular, but many people would say it was a price worth paying for full employment. Over a number of years significant changes in the impact of taxes and spending do take place, so we should not dismiss this type of policy option simply because the numbers involved are big.

The benefit system and minimum wages

In the UK, unlike many other industrial countries, the ratio of unemployment benefits to wages has been falling since the 1960s. If the rates of benefit were to be cut that might well reduce the numbers of claimants but at the expense of increased poverty for those who remain out of work. Most people would consider this a price *not* worth paying.

The replacement ratio could also be reduced however by paying benefits to workers on low pay, which would of course tend to reduce poverty rather than to increase it. Family Credit already does this and the scheme has many admirers. Some would like to develop this approach much further and make it a major element in a strategy to achieve full employment. Certainly it merits careful examination and it is possible that it is the best option available.

As compared with the alternative of reforming NI contributions and employment subsidies considered above it has two disadvantages. The first is simply that it approaches the main problem we are concerned with indirectly rather than directly, by focusing on individual or household income when it should focus on job creation. The second disadvantage, to my mind at least, is that most of the schemes considered require some form of means test for the individual or the household so as to keep down their cost. A relationship of dependency is unavoidable between the recipients and the state as the donor. This may be right and proper as a temporary relationship for individuals or households in times of particular adversity, but it is not so appropriate as a permanent relationship between the state and perhaps millions of less skilled workers. I do not think that Beveridge would have approved at all.

The attraction of paying benefits to those in work reflects the increase in the dispersion of wages over the past decade, adding to the prevalence of low pay, often of pay so low that workers gain little compared to their benefit entitlements. The same increase in dispersion has not been observed in much of continental Europe, partly because of minimum wage regulations.

Where minimum wages are high relative to rates of benefit they must reduce the possibility of creating relatively low paid jobs for relatively low skilled workers. The countries concerned therefore face a difficult choice between better pay and more jobs, with a conflict of interest between the employed and the unemployed to be resolved. The issue has, of course, been much discussed in this country in recent months and I do not think I have much to add to the debate. The main issue so far as unemployment is concerned is not whether there should be a minimum wage or not, but the level at which the minimum is set if we do have one. If it was set high enough to require the wages now paid to a large number of workers to be raised, then some, though not all, of the jobs concerned would be lost.

The situation could be helped by the reforms to national insurance contributions or the introduction of employment subsidies already discussed. By cutting total unit wage costs for those offering relatively low skilled jobs the incidence of very low pay should be reduced. The need for minimum wage regulation would then be less, and so also would be the loss of jobs if a minimum wage was in fact introduced.

Education and Training

I have left until last what is perhaps the ideal solution to the problem of unemployment. If only we could make the labour force more productive, then of course the economy would be more competitive, real wages and living standards would rise, and the prospects for employment would improve as well. Everyone is in favour of better education and training, for these reasons and many more.

In the context of structural unemployment however, we should look not just at the average level of education and training but at its variation across the work-force. It is striking that in this country the variation of educational achievement is greater than in most other European countries. In the context of the distribution of 'earning power' and its relation to unemployment this is an important and disturbing fact. The widening seems to begin at an early age, with very different rates of progress of children at primary school. It may then be self-reinforcing as the children who have not benefited fully from one stage in their education get left further and further behind. It is also true that in this country we have been relatively good at providing higher education opportunities for the academic elite and relatively bad at organising craft training or vocational qualifications for the population at large. Public awareness of these issues has increased over the past ten years and new policies have been introduced. New initiatives have been announced within the last few months. This is not the occasion for a critique, but the intention behind these reforms is clearly to address long-standing problems that have contributed to the high level of unemployment in Britain.

In reviewing the various forms of policy action which might help reduce unemployment we must keep in mind the very different time horizons over which they might be effective. The reform of education and training for the population as a whole will mainly affect the employment opportunities of the next generation. That does not make them any the less important or urgent, but it means that on their own they are not a sufficient response to unemployment today. If the Government made a commitment to full employment it would be reasonable to ask to what time period the commitment referred. If the answer was well into the twenty-first century, then the popular endorsement would not be so enthusiastic.

Conclusions

It is remarkable how support of the objective of full employment has survived despite the failure for over twenty years to achieve it. Clearly it accords with a popular perception of the responsibility of the State and the well-being of society. Self-interest may also be involved now that so few people can feel really secure in their possession of jobs. The concerns which led to the commitment made in the 1944 White Paper are no less relevant today. A job is still, for most people, the basis for participation in the community, and to be deprived of a job is to be rejected or pushed to the margins.

The full employment of the post-war period reflected a condition of persistent excess demand in the labour market in which inflation was suppressed by regulation and by restraint in the use of market power. It also depended on a consensus, not just between political parties about the conduct of policy, but also between employers and employees about the priority of jobs as against pay.

Those tacit agreements broke down in the 1960s and attempts to replace them with the formal structure of prices and incomes policies have all been unsuccessful. Structural unemployment has developed for a combination of reasons, which include the lasting effects of three severe recessions, a lack of flexibility in relative rates of pay, and a widening in the dispersion of potential earnings within the labour force. Since 1979 (but not only because of the change in government) the British economy has been transformed from a largely corporatist to a free-market system. This is the context within which a new commitment to full employment would now be made.

It would be a cruel deception to speak of full employment as an objective if there were no way of achieving it. My own view is that full employment is possible, although only at a considerable cost. Some form of taxation would have to be increased or some form of public expenditure cut. The sums involved could be large. The question remains therefore whether political support can be found in the country for the measures which would be needed. There is no lack of support for the objective, but the real challenge is to build support for a sustained effort over many years and for some sacrifice in the interests of social solidarity.

Steady, non-cyclical, growth, if it can be achieved, would be a great help, but on its own it will not result in full employment. A successful industrial policy, if that can be achieved, would also be of value both in supporting real wages and escaping from a balance of payments constraint. The employment problem could be greatly eased by improvements in education and training, and for the long-term this is the most attractive solution. But the group most likely to be helped by such reforms would consist of new entrants to the labour force, so as a means of achieving full employment this may take us well into the next century.

Special employment measures, targeted on the unemployed themselves, to improve their job prospects on an individual basis, will always be of value if they are well-designed. But they cannot be expected to cope with mass unemployment as we have known it since the 1970s. Extending them to a much larger scale would run the risk of creating another form of marginalisation, not very different in its social implications from unemployment itself.

In a market economy the main instrument for increasing job opportunities for those at risk of unemployment should be incentives and relative costs. These can be influenced by changes in the system of national insurance contributions, changes in income taxation or public spending on transfers and subsidies. The reforms needed to bring about full employment by this method would be on a large scale and involve substantial costs to the general taxpayer. It is best to aim as directly as possible at the objective of creating more jobs, and for that reason reform of national insurance contributions and subsidies for low-skill employment seem more appropriate than benefits paid to low income individuals or households. They also avoid the intrusiveness, and the sense of dependency, which is always associated with a means test. They would have to be introduced gradually, and the scale of change needed could not be calculated accurately in advance. Suppose however that the reform was continued to the point where the cost of employing the lowest-paid workers fell mainly on the community as a whole rather than on the employer. If one went to that extreme then I have little doubt that full employment would be the result.

There may be other means of reaching the same objective, not covered in this paper. I hope I will have provoked some of my professional colleagues to continue the debate by responding to what I have said. I hope that most of them would agree that full employment is a very worthwhile aim, and that, given a high priority, it is an aim that we *can* achieve.

CHAPTER 3

The challenge: working together towards full employment

JOHN MONKS, General Secretary, TUC

HOWARD DAVIES, Director General, CBI

The Right Hon DAVID HUNT, MBE, MP,
Secretary of State for Employment

Questions and Answers

JOHN MONKS, General Secretary, TUC

This conference is a unique occasion. We have sought to bring together the various original supporting organisations of the 1944 White Paper, and to ask them, 50 years on, to address once again the issue of full employment.

The essential strength of the commitment in 1944 was that it was a shared commitment. The TUC itself had been pressing the cause of full employment for many years previously. On a Government Committee in the 1930s, Ernest Bevin was Keynes' only ally. But over the next decade and in the unique circumstances of wartime Britain, Bevin was able to provide the political muscle to secure the widespread acceptance of the work of Keynes and Beveridge – an acceptance which underpinned British economic policy well into the 1970s.

The decision to hold this conference has attracted opposition. Many people remember the policies of excessive monetarism and the effect that has had on unemployment. Phrases like 'a price worth paying' have burned into the flesh, leaving deep scars.

They remember the loss of jobs in manufacturing since 1979 – three million fewer now than then – the fastest rate of decline among the European nations.

They remember the harsh and precipitate pit closures and the deep void that remains today in the coalfield communities.

They remember the decision to end the link between benefits and average earnings, and the resulting increase in poverty.

They remember too the seven Acts of Parliament which have provided great freedom to employers in the British labour market to a degree unique in the

European Union, while at the same time more and more restrictions have been imposed on British unions.

They remember last summer's removal of minimum wages for two and a half million low paid workers, while forcing unions to have to re-sign the six million members who pay their dues on the check-off system.

They remember the denigration of the concept of public service and the depiction at times of public servants as being in some kind of sheltered employment.

They remember this, and more – *and so do I.* We hold this conference against the background of deep divisions, sharp hostilities, and a decade and a half of mutual suspicion.

Yet for me that makes the occasion all the more important. The countries which come nearest to full employment are those which have built a consensus and commitment to common action, a commitment which survives political change and is a consistent theme of Government policy, supported by key opposition parties, employers and effective unions.

The TUC does not approach today's conference with a glib plan. We don't say we can get to full employment if you adopt this 10 point plan or that particular five point charter. What we do say is that we stand ready again to be a partner in the *pursuit* of full employment.

We are clear about the issues to be addressed. I will present a series of challenges to the other participants and to ask for the challenges to be addressed, and addressed in a spirit of partnership.

My *first* challenge to the other participants is to ask:

'Do you believe that full employment should be a central goal of economic policy?'; and

'Do you believe that full employment is a practicable goal over the medium term?'.

There are those who do not regard full employment as a central goal. Like Andrew Britton, I have been re-reading Beveridge and at the heart of the matter is an ethical and moral judgment about how we treat individuals in the labour market and in society.

Few however would answer *no* to the question about desirability, though I suspect in the early 1980s gung ho monetarists might have been proud to have made control of inflation the only goal of economic policy.

There is, as a result of that, strong suspicion in trade union circles that mass unemployment has been a deliberate act of policy to weaken unions, collective bargaining and real wages.

However, I suspect many are in the camp of wishing the desirability of full employment, but doubting its feasibility.

But the fact is that unless society can provide work, and quality work with decent pay and conditions, all the concerns we have about current social problems will multiply, as the gaps widen between rich and poor, and between those in quality work and those outside.

All the problems which stem from unemployment and poverty, or which are worsened by them – crime, homelessness, family breakdown – would get bigger in scale. A failure of the political mainstream to deliver would result in despair, opening the door again to the dark forces of totalitarianism, racism and narrow nationalism.

We really have no choice but to rise to the challenge of adopting full employment as our shared objective.

My *second* challenge is in the field of macroeconomics. Low inflation is an important goal of policy, but there is more room, much more room, for the management of demand to prompt growth than has been recognised in recent times. It is an inescapable fact that the economy must grow above the two-and-a-half per cent trend to get unemployment down.

The crude reality is that productivity is growing at an average of two per cent each year, and two per cent economic growth would only provide a standstill overall in jobs. We have lost 1.4 million jobs since 1990 which shows what happens when growth has been zero or even minus in some years.

Now we will *not* create the three million or so jobs by demand management alone. There are constraints on one nation acting alone in this area. But the neglect of economic management must be corrected and advantage taken of the current conditions of low inflation, excess capacity, and the pick up of the European recovery.

In this area, why do not the Government and the CBI sign up to the Delors White Paper? Jacques Delors had originally agreed to come to this conference to put his case, but an important meeting with Chancellor Kohl about the start of the German Presidency has intervened. President Delors is arguing for a target to be set – the goal of reducing unemployment in the European Union by half by the year 2000. Even then, that would leave a rate of five per cent, unacceptably high by the standard we became used to until the 1970s, but a massive improvement on what we now have. And the Delors Plan envisaged a major boost to demand, powered by some big transnational projects aimed at improving European infrastructure and our ability to compete – projects which would not incidentally have been charged against Britain's public sector deficit.

What is wrong with that?

The way the Delors Plan has so far been shuffled off the table by the Finance Ministers is a tragic error and I urge the Government to return to it without their Euro-sceptic glasses on.

I also urge the Government to follow-up interesting ideas that are emerging about public/private finance for large projects and to allow the use of local authority capital receipts for new building.

My *third* challenge is about the nature of the labour market needed for full employment.

Do we choose the de-regulated, low welfare model traditionally associated with the USA, but about which it is evident that the current US Government is dissatisfied? Or do we choose the 'European Union' model, combining a more regulated labour market and reasonable welfare provision? Government Ministers tend to claim the former is friendly to employment while the latter is a recipe for unemployment. The Secretary of State himself took this approach at the Jobs Summit in Detroit recently.

The UK has spent the past 15 years moving in the direction of a US style labour market with cuts in protection in the labour market (most recently the abolition of the minimum rate fixing wage councils) and restrictions on unions, while attempting to maintain something resembling a European Welfare State.

This view was recently spelt out by the Chancellor of the Exchequer in his Mais lecture where he proclaimed his belief that the objective should be to combine American enterprise and free market efficiency with the European commitment to the welfare state.

Well, I say to him – watch what happens to public spending if some employers can continue to shift the cost of subsistence onto the State. It will continue to soar.

The pay-off of deregulating policies in terms of jobs in the UK has been nothing like as strong as in the USA. And most of the jobs created have been part-time while full-time job opportunities have shrunk, especially drastically for men with relatively low skill attainments. At the same time, earnings have become more unequal.

At the moment, our work and welfare model seems to be giving us the worst of both worlds – more poor people in work and also a high level of welfare dependency. Employers are using their freedom to impose employment patterns – casualised patterns with, for example, no sick pay, no pensions, no security – to shift extra burdens onto the welfare state. Lower pay levels for example result in more claimants for family income supplements and housing benefit.

The response of some on the Right is to argue for more de-regulation and a slashing of welfare. Those tempted down that path ought to reflect that the US Government have already been there, seen it, and did not like what it produced.

That Government is seeking, especially through Robert Reich, the US Labour Secretary, to take a new path – one leading to more jobs but also good jobs – ones which are skilled and well paid.

The European Union too is also looking for a path which creates jobs and maintains social solidarity – the cohesion of communities – a path in which flexibility is defined in a manner more friendly to working families and women.

We should remember Beveridge's wise words in 1994. I quote:

'the labour market should always be a seller's market rather than a buyer's market . . . a person who cannot sell his labour is in effect told that he is of no use'.

Facing up to the competitive challenge means looking afresh at the various stakeholders in companies, looking for ways to boost investment through the tax treatment of company earnings as both Robin Cook (Shadow Trade and Industry Spokesperson) and Stephen Dorrell (Financial Secretary to the Treasury) have suggested, and encouraging long-termism in corporate decision making.

This, I believe, makes it crucial that this country moves to adopt labour market policies in line with the European Social Chapter. British employers should start to get the message that competitiveness cannot in our context be based on low wages, low skills and low performance – not, anyway, while maintaining social cohesion and any real sense of shared experiences in our communities. Many of them know that but too many do not.

The Social Chapter is not unfriendly to jobs and competitiveness. My message today is that quality jobs underpin competitiveness.

Now there are deep divisions on this platform about this issue and about the related issue of a national minimum wage which we believe is essential to stop some employers enforcing poverty wages in the process and shifting the cost of subsistence onto the welfare state. But I hope that the participants at this conference will recognise that de-regulated labour markets lead to widening income distribution and social inequality, to less people receiving training as more and more jobs become casualised, and not least to inefficiency.

My *fourth* challenge – and over which there is a much greater degree of agreement – concerns the need to improve *training*. It is now commonplace to hear that this nation, and others, have only one resource – the skills and ingenuity of the people. It is equally commonplace for us all to recognise that Britain's record on education and training has been relatively poor.

We have the training targets agreed by the CBI and the TUC and supported by the Government; we are supporting the system of national vocational qualifications. We are active too in prompting the Investors in People Initiative. And we claim some of the credit for the recent welcome launch by the Government of modern apprenticeships. We want to be *partners* in the delivery of these schemes.

We do differ on one important training matter. I do not believe that enough employers will train adequately unless some stick is added to the existing carrots. And today we urge others to support our appeal for a modern training levy, perhaps payable by employers if Investors in People status is not achieved within a given time.

My *fifth* challenge concerns the treatment of the unemployed. Let me make it plain. I do not believe that lowering benefits to force people to take low paid jobs is acceptable. It is demeaning and insulting.

Work is central to people's lives. It is important to help the unemployed in all ways possible to get back to work. I note the Government are gearing up to make welfare reform a key theme in the next Parliamentary session. But a Scrooge-like approach to cutting unemployment benefit from 12 months to six months, and requiring the jobless to keep making greater efforts to find work is cruelty, especially when there is a widespread shortage of jobs.

A better approach would be to provide good temporary work programmes and training schemes with decent allowances particularly aimed at the long-term unemployed and young people. We know from the old Manpower Services Commission (MSC) schemes that there was no problem of take up on those. The problem was meeting demand.

We are also interested in ideas about in-work help such as employment subsidies or widening of family credit style benefits. These could help, although the Government must guard against subsidising employers offering lousy pay and conditions, and taking advantage of both their employees *and* the State.

41

There is one central theme behind my challenges. I believe the heart of the full employment debate is how we engender a greater sense of solidarity. A fine old trade union word – solidarity – but we use it today outside our traditional context of supporting each other in disputes.

Solidarity in this context is recognising that the countries with the best employment records have been the ones with social and economic institutions, including strong trade unions, that have allowed success in the internationally competitive sector to be shared across the economy.

The countries and companies that are going to be successful in the future are not going to be those which have undermined the employer/employee relationship with casualisation and imposed part-time working. That will not deliver competitively in the long-term.

And the more productive we are, the more jobs we must create.

We have launched a debate on how to rebuild solidarity in the fiercely competitive world of the 1990s, how we can work together for full employment, despite our differences. The papers and proceedings from this conference will form the basis of a TUC programme for full employment. Can I add my thanks to all those who have contributed already. The TUC will be consulting widely on its proposals both inside and outside the trade union Movement and keeping full employment at the very heart of economic and political debates.

This anniversary of the 1944 White Paper therefore is one of those occasions when an anniversary provides a valuable reference point for contemporary debate. Can we rediscover the collective will and commitment to take up the challenge of making full employment as relevant in the Britain of the 1990's as it was in the 1940's. It won't be the same as in 1944. Technological change is accelerating. New social patterns are emerging.

The increasing demand for quality work from women and pressure for family friendly employment supports must be recognised. But I repeat, we can together, build full employment into post-cold war reconstruction just as we did into post-war reconstruction.

That is *my* challenge to you *all*.

HOWARD DAVIES, Director General, CBI

I would like to begin by congratulating the TUC on organising this conference.

First, I think it was a good idea to set the proceedings for today in a human context, by beginning with the experiences of some individual unemployed people themselves. It is quite easy to slip into talking about unemployment in a purely statistical and econometric way, yet to most people it is the human dimension of unemployment which most affects them.

A second important contribution which the conference has made already is through the background papers, which are excellent and which, taken together, significantly improved my understanding of the issues. The downside is that they rather ruined my weekend. Because I had planned to speak in a general way about the state of the recovery, and the most promising sectors for employment growth. Instead, I think it might be more helpful to you if I gave a direct response to the challenges in the papers, summarised in John Philpott's helpful overview (see Chapter 5).

So I will address three main subjects:

–   First, whether full employment is a useful policy aim;

–   Secondly, in the light of my answer to that question, what specific policy measures might now be appropriate to try to bring unemployment down;

–   and Third, what the employer contribution should be.

But I would like, briefly, to make one contextual point. Perhaps because I spend a good portion of my own time wrestling with European policy issues, I did find the papers, collectively, somewhat Anglo-centric in focus. It is important to recognise that the problem we face in the UK is one which affects all of our Community partners. Indeed, some of them would say that their problem is worse than ours. While UK unemployment last year was, at 10.3 per cent, above the OECD average, it was below the EC average of 10.6 per cent. And, in contrast with all other EC countries, our unemployment peak in the last recession was below the peak in the early 1980's recession.

In pointing to those facts, I do not mean to argue that the problem has been solved and that you can all go home and worry instead about the forthcoming series against the South Africans. But I do think it is important to begin with an objective assessment of the strengths and weaknesses of the UK labour market.

The recent OECD *Jobs Study* provides such an assessment. In the section on the United Kingdom they note, on the positive side, that:

- The average employment ratio for the UK is about four percentage points above the OECD average;

- That there has been a steady rise in the female participation rate;

- There was an impressive decline in relative and absolute youth unemployment in the second half of the 1980s;

- Measures such as the Re-Start Programme contributed to a rapid decline in the long-term unemployment ratio in the late 1980s; and

- That far-reaching structural reforms make the UK labour market more flexible than most others in Europe.

On the other hand, they note that:

- Our skill base remains weak;

- They are somewhat critical of TECs and LECs, whose performance so far they describe as having "fallen short of initial expectations";

- Once again, the long-term unemployed have a low probability of finding a job;

- They criticise the indefinite duration of income support;

- They also argue that real wage rigidity remains both a public and private sector problem, saying that "notwithstanding our unemployment over the last three years, public sector pay has risen faster than private sector pay"; and

- They note that earnings dispersion increased dramatically during the 1980s.

There are aspects of this assessment with which the CBI might differ. We are rather more positive about what the TECs have done, for example. And I am inclined to think that the rapid growth in earnings dispersion is emerging as a more serious social and economic problem than is yet appreciated by most politicians. But, overall, the OECD's is a balanced assessment.

Full employment as a policy aim

Let me now turn, then, to the question of full employment. Is full employment a useful policy objective?

I am tempted to say that this is a political question, and to decline to answer it. Even leaving the Government out of count for the time being (and David Hunt can answer for himself), the three Labour leadership contenders have adopted different formulations of their employment aims, and Paddy Ashdown of the Liberal Democrats has strongly criticised the idea of using full employment as a policy objective. Yet I would not question the strong commitment of all four to putting a reduction in unemployment at the top of their priorities.

So I do not think it is sensible to erect the test of a commitment to full employment, in precisely those words, as a politically correct litmus test.

The strongest arguments for a commitment to full employment are that it might raise the profile of unemployment as an economic and social problem, might provide encouragement to unemployed people by emphasising the aim of social inclusion, rather than implying that the unemployed perform some economic function only through their exclusion from work, and it might spur innovation and fruitful experimentation in policy making. These are not inconsiderable arguments.

On the other hand, since it is not clear that anyone has a very clear idea of how to get to full employment, or even how to define it, a Government targeting full employment as its prime policy objective might be condemned to disappointing itself, and unemployed people themselves. Failure would certainly quickly negate some of the positive arguments I have outlined. And there is a clear risk that such failure might lead to inappropriate short-term policy responses. In particular, a government targeting full employment might be tempted to engage in short-term demand expansion which might bring damaging long-term consequences for inflation, competitiveness and growth. Along with Andrew Britton, we do not believe that the problem of unemployment can be solved by stimulating aggregate demand on its own.

The CBI is not, thank goodness, about to write an election manifesto. But if we did I think we would be unlikely to include a commitment to full employment, in those terms. We would advocate a commitment to stable financial conditions (something the Government ought to be able to achieve), combined with a strong supply side, or competitiveness policy, to maximise the growth potential of the economy.

But if a government with a policy commitment to full employment were elected we would not take our bat home.

Employers do believe that we should strive to create an economic environment in which there are jobs available for all those with the motivation and the aptitudes to add value. And it is clear that we are not in that happy position at the moment. Which brings me to my second subject, what is to be done?

What more can be done to increase employment?

We have been giving further thought recently, in the CBI, to the problem of unemployment, as the recovery proceeds. That is because, again like Andrew Britton (see Chapter 2), we are somewhat pessimistic about the employment prospect. We are therefore undertaking some studies, which will come to fruition around the time of our National Conference in November so, in that sense, this conference is not ideally timed for us.

But I can give you an idea of the way our thinking is evolving. At some points I will describe 'CBI policy'. At others it may be more a case of musings by me. In our case there is a clear distinction. We are a democratic organisation with lots of properly constituted committees. No all powerful, life-time contract General-Secretaries for us.

Since there is no one cause of our high unemployment rate, there is no one cure for it. That is the first, and maybe the last, point on which we can all reach agreement. In our view there are nine areas in which progress could and should be made, proceeding from the general to the particular.

Nine responses

(a) *Productivity and competitiveness.* First, whatever else we do, we must not lose sight of the fact that the key to increased prosperity for everyone is productivity improvement and enhanced competitiveness. That is true in all sectors of the economy, but I was particularly pleased to see a paper on manufacturing in the conference documentation. The piece by Greenhalgh and Gregory is very much in line with the views of our National Manufacturing Council.

I do not propose to labour the competitiveness point today. We have done so, many times. I would just make one point. It is vital not to give the impression that more employment is somehow in conflict with enhancing competitiveness. Employers are most acutely aware of competitive pressures on them, pressures which now often act very quickly indeed. That drives most of their actions. If you want to engage employers in the battle against unemployment, you must show that it works with the grain of increased productivity and competitiveness. That is not impossible to do, but unions and others have often not positioned themselves in that way in the past. Indeed not all politicians on the left do so even now.

(b) *Monetary and fiscal policy.* The second area in which progress needs to be made is macroeconomic and especially fiscal policy. It may seem odd for me to include that in the list when I have already dismissed the notion of a demand management approach targeted specifically at full employment. But the level and composition of public spending are important. The level is, in our view, too high – largely because of unemployment. And the balance between taxation and borrowing, and between investment and consumption, is also crucial.

We would completely agree with John Philpott (see Chapter 5) when he says that "society will have to face up to the fact that investment – private and public – in industrial capacity and in people – must take priority over consumption for a period of years". It is why we have been prepared to support tax increases, and to resist panicky calls by Conservative backbenchers for tax cuts. The Government needs to go further with – on the one hand – more incentives for the private sector to invest and, on the other, a shift in the composition of public spending towards investment. In the housing area, for example, I favour a switch back from consumption subsidies, to bricks and mortar subsidy. That would mean switching mortgage interest relief, and some of the pressures pushing up rents and housing benefits at the same time, to construction grants through the Housing Corporation. That would generate employment in the construction industry, employment which is particularly suitable for men with lower skills.

It means, too, more private investment in public sector projects. I sit on the Private Finance Panel which is proving to be a difficult but ultimately fulfilling exercise. More could be done. And I am glad that the Labour Party is also in favour of moves in that direction. It would be good to hear more from unions on the subject, too.

(c) *Wages.* In the number three slot, the graveyard of English batsmen over the years, I put wages. As William Brown (see Chapter 5 and Annex B) says "hopes of full employment . . . are forlorn unless labour costs per unit of output can be kept in line with those of our competitors". And even now, wages are rising more rapidly here than in most other developed economies.

Pay determination has been an Achilles heel of the UK economy for decades. There are some signs, in this recovery, that lessons may have been learned, but there remains a problem. We have, as William Brown describes, reached a kind of halfway house between centralised and local bargaining, which may not deliver the optimum result. We have a poor example being set from the top of many companies, and there are still unions who think it is cute to launch macho double figure claims as a sign of industrial virility. Unless pay increases are kept below the rate of productivity improvement in this recovery, our unemployment problem will get worse.

(d) *Training*. We are making progress in the skills revolution though we will not meet all the education and training targets by the end of the decade unless our efforts are increased in both intensity and quality.

And there is a particular issue here in relation to unemployed people. An employer-led training policy, which we support, may not be optimally designed from the perspective of the long-term unemployed, or even of those who move in and out of the labour market. A more flexible labour market may need a more flexible training policy to match.

We are looking at that now. We are surveying employers about the skills of the unemployed who present themselves for work, and we shall be surveying unemployed people themselves to assess their perception of the training opportunities open to them.

Our hypothesis is that some changes may be needed to allow people to continue to upskill themselves during periods of temporary unemployment. There may be a need for more suitable work experience opportunities for the unemployed. Or it might be appropriate to expand training credits to ensure that those who are currently out of the labour market retain some market power. One way or another, we need to improve the connections between the long-term unemployed and the training market, as well as the labour market.

My remaining points are more directly related to experiences of the unemployed, and the particular difficulties they face in getting into the labour market. They might be grouped loosely under the heading 'Lowering the barriers to work'.

(e) *Childcare*. The first is the problem of childcare. It may seem perverse to begin there, in the light of the rapid expansion of female participation over the last decade. But not all of that increased female participation has been on women's own terms. And, as Patricia Hewitt shows in her paper, it has been concentrated among the partners of working men (see Chapter 5 and Annex B). Indeed some two thirds of partners of working men are in work, compared to only a quarter of the partners of unemployed men. Part of the answer lies in the operation of the benefits system. But there is also the cost and availability of childcare to consider. This is a particularly acute problem, of course, for lone parents.

Some progress has been made, and we welcome the earnings disregard introduced in the last Budget. But I think that more is almost certainly needed. One option we favour is the extension of tax relief for workplace nurseries to the provision of all employer funded childcare. Workplace nurseries are not always a good answer, particularly not in London, and the restriction of tax relief to them only is a handicap to the development of employment opportunities suitable for lone parents.

There are other issues, too, around the general subject of 'family friendly' working policies which are of great significance. Patricia Hewitt describes them in her paper. They relate to men as well as to women. And there is an interaction here with the broader question of the appropriate distribution of working time in the economy. While I have some doubts about the more far-reaching proposals for work sharing which Paul Ormerod canvasses (see Chapter 5 and Annex B), I do think it right, as Patricia Hewitt says, to try to "enable both women and men to pursue more flexible working lives, in which earning and caring can be shared between them". If that does result in some people, by choice, working less – and earning less – then it could be part of the solution to the unemployment problem.

(f) *Discrimination.* One especially disappointing feature of the last recession was that after a period during which unemployment rates in ethnic minorities had been converging on the rate for the white population as a whole, they began to diverge again in the early 1990s.

This aspect of the unemployment problem was given only cursory attention in the papers for the conference, though it is mentioned by David Piachaud (see Chapter 5 and Annex B). Perhaps that is because neither the causes nor the solutions of this problem are clear. Part of the reason for the changing trend may be that employers have been operating a kind of LIFO – last in first out – principle. Also, unemployment is heavily spatially concentrated in inner city areas with higher ethnic populations. And some ethnic minorities are, on average, less well qualified than the population as a whole, though that clearly does not apply to the Indian or Chinese communities. But undoubtedly ethnic minorities also face casual discrimination as an additional barrier to entry to employment. This is an area for further examination, in our view, and we welcome the new campaign promoted by the Commission for Racial Equality which began last week.

The last three areas relate particularly to the long-term unemployed, rightly seen by the authors of most of the conference papers, as the core of the problem.

(g) *Counselling.* There is some evidence that direct intervention with the long-term unemployed, advising them on how to get back in touch with the labour market, can be effective. Such programmes can be expensive but the case for supporting them looks to be a strong one; it is supported by the OECD.

(h) *Targeted wage subsidies.* Another area recommended by the OECD, and where the Government have already been experimenting, is in the provision of targeted wage subsidies to employers to induce them to take on the long-term unemployed. This is not an easy area in which to operate. The practical requirement is for a subsidy rate which is high enough to overcome employers' prejudices about the value and risks of taking on the long-term unemployed, but not so high as to induce artificial labour churning.

500 employers have participated in the pilot schemes being undertaken at the moment. Anecdotal evidence from them suggests that the vacancies on offer required skill levels which many scheme participants could not match. So there is a loop back from job subsidies to the training needs of the long-term unemployed, which is not surprising. But I think there is the germ of a successful idea here. I hope the Government find resources to expand it.

(i) *Benefits.* The other side of the coin of direct job subsidies is the benefit system. Here we enter a kind of crystal maze of traps, tapers, withdrawals and disregards, a maze from which many unemployed people find it hard to escape. Life inside the maze, while not exactly a life of Riley, can seem more predictable and in some ways more secure than the uncertain job market. Richard Layard argues that the main reason for the higher prevalence of long-term unemployment in Europe is "almost incontrovertible: it is the long duration for which unemployment benefits are payable" (see Chapter 5 and Annex B).

The OECD conclusion on this subject is that "countries should legislate for only moderate levels of benefits, maintain effective checks on eligibility, and guarantee places on active programmes as a substitute for paying massive income support indefinitely". They also argue that the transition from income support to work should be made more financially attractive.

These general principles are sensible, though fiendishly difficult to work through in practice. But I believe there are some practical ideas around, which the Government would do well to consider. It is increasingly widely accepted that the principle of extending in-work benefits beyond those who

50

now receive Family Credit is one worthy of support. Nigel Lawson argued that case in a recent lecture. He links it to worries about the impact of global competition on the incomes of the unskilled. That is a concern I very much share.

The Government have already moved to ease the transition from unemployment to work in certain ways, by allowing some part-time earnings to be disregarded. But, again, I think the case for moving further is quite strong. For example, it might be possible to introduce separate earnings disregards for unemployed people and their partners, to reduce the disincentive for the partners of unemployed men to take part-time work, or one might allow unused weekly earnings disregards to be accumulated as an earnings credit to be used in one go if required, making the transition to work financially easier.

Are these ideas politically realistic? I do not see why not. In their papers submitted to the Detroit Jobs Summit earlier this year, the Government referred to the need to look carefully at the interface between the tax and benefit systems to ensure that appropriate incentives were in place. Those incentives are not strong at the moment.

The employers' role in combating unemployment

My last subject is the role of employers. What should it be?

The main contributions you should look for from employers are entrepreneurship and innovation. If we could breed more entrepreneurs, that would do as much as anything to enhance job opportunities for the unemployed and wealth creation for us all.

But employers have other responsibilities, too. They should also play their part in ensuring that the benefits of productivity improvement do not go exclusively to insiders, whether at the top or bottom of the earnings distribution, and they should look for opportunities to expand. One of the unfortunate inheritances from two deep recessions within the living memories of most of our board members is a high degree of caution, particularly about expanding employment. Employers are nervous about being caught out, once again, with surplus capacity which is expensive and painful to remove.

We are not likely soon to return to the days when employers assessed their own personal worth by the numbers of people they employed. But I hope we can return to a position where large companies are not afraid to hire. The recent upsurge in job advertisements suggests that that process of correction may be beginning to occur.

You should also expect employers to lead on training. And where they do not, it is reasonable for unions to press them to do so. Companies which will not commit themselves to becoming Investors in People, for example, deserve pressure from below.

Employers can take a lead, too, in building bridges between the employed and the unemployed populations through Employees in the Community schemes.

And, centrally, it is reasonable for you to look to the CBI for a view on unemployment and what should be done about it. Certainly our Employment Policy Committee puts a higher priority on its unemployment related work at present than on proposing new and exciting reforms of employment law. That may not be true of all bodies representing employers, however.

Lastly, I think it is reasonable to expect employers to participate in public discussions of this kind with trade unions and with the Government. I am pleased to see David Hunt on this platform with us. It may be that he and I will be criticised, as John Monks has already been, for gesture politics, or for supping with too short handled a spoon. I believe such arguments should be very strongly resisted. Some of the decisions which need to be taken if we are to bring unemployment down will be painful for someone, whether it be unemployed people, benefit recipients, or even unions themselves. Those difficult decisions will only be possible if there is a high degree of public understanding of the need for them, and some basis of consent.

We are not going to be back in the business of tripartite deals. They didn't work in the past, and the structures which didn't work then are even weaker now.

I do, however, see positive value in what, when we meet in Brussels, we call the Social Dialogue, though of course we would not dream of using such a term here.

The Right Hon. DAVID HUNT, MBE, MP, Secretary of State for Employment

May I welcome the holding of this conference at the Headquarters of the TUC and say that I welcome the opportunity of a positive and constructive dialogue.

In the developed world all governments agree that the greatest economic policy issue we face is unemployment.

The OECD *Jobs Study* echoes the conclusions reached at the European Council and the G7 Jobs Conference in Detroit. There, I set out five principles behind a strategy for jobs:

- a stable economic environment;

- encouragement for self-employment and enterprise;

- a better balance between the rights of those in work and the needs of those out of work;

- investment in skills and qualifications;

- positive help for unemployed people to get back to work.

I want to see policies which aim towards full employment in a successful modern society.

Building on those five principles let me respond immediately to the first challenge that John Monk's threw out (see page 37). Let me make it absolutely clear that as Secretary of State for Employment I want to see policies which aim towards full employment in a successful modern society.

Full employment

Full employment has been a shared aim in Britain since Beveridge wrote his famous report *Full Employment in a Free Society*, 50 years ago. The 1994 White Paper on Employment Policy stated that:

"The Government accept as one of their primary aims and responsibilities the maintenance of a high and stable level of employment after the war".

The same White Paper went on to say:

"employment cannot be created by Act of Parliament or by Government action alone. Government policy will be directed to bringing conditions favourable to the maintenance of a high level of employment".

So the answer to your challenge is *yes*. As Secretary of State for Employment – I believe *any* Secretary of State for Employment – I want to see full employment.

As John Major said not so long ago, "every Prime Minister wishes to achieve full employment". And some of you will know my background. My home city of Liverpool and Merseyside, that is where I live, that is where my constituency is, that is where I have learned that long, high and sustained levels of unemployment can do much to undermine the social fabric of society. So I want to see full employment. Disagreement consists only in how we achieve that shared goal. It is not much use advocating full employment whilst at the same time pressing for policies which would destroy jobs.

The serious nature of the challenge faced by Europe is illustrated starkly by the figures. Unemployment is now about 20 million in the European Union – more than one in ten Europeans are now out of work.

Although in the last 18 months unemployment in the UK has fallen by 310,000, over the same period the totals have increased by 1.9 million in the rest of Europe. Germany alone has more than three and a half million people out of work and France nearly as many.

For young people the figures are particularly bad. Over 20% – one in five – of Europe's young people are unemployed; 15.1 per cent in the UK. In some of the more inflexible economies of Europe the figures are truly horrendous:

24 per cent of young people in France are unemployed;

32 per cent in Italy; and

38 per cent in Spain.

In Europe temporary or casual work is also now very much a feature of modern economies. Although in the UK just seven per cent of jobs are temporary, one of the lowest rates in the EU, in Europe the average has risen to over 10 per cent and in Spain the percentage of employees in temporary or casual jobs has risen to over 30 per cent.

How is unemployment to be brought down?

We need to ask ourselves why it is that Europe has such high levels of unemployment. What is it that differentiates Europe from other trading blocs?

The answer is very simple – Europe has failed to create the jobs our people need. Since 1971 employment in the USA has grown by 45 per cent – an extra 37 million jobs. In Europe over the same period the increase was less than 10 per cent – only 11 million jobs, and most of those were in the public sector. That is Europe's problem – jobless growth.

Where will the jobs come from?

There are two very popular political banners at the moment – competitiveness and full employment.

Nobody is actually *against* either: I am certainly in favour of both, and I think it is important to emphasise the connection between them: they are in fact two sides of the same coin. There is only one way in which living standards will rise and more jobs will be created. As a nation we must produce more and sell more. And we must do so in an increasingly competitive world.

So how can we make Britain and Europe more competitive so that we can keep pace with other nations which are only too happy to take market share given the chance?

The answer is we must compete in a global market place.

The challenge is how to turn this to our advantage. To see the Asian Tigers not as a threat, but as new markets for our goods and services. Many British companies have already risen spectacularly to this challenge. In the first three months of this year, for example, British exports to China were worth £218 million – 47 per cent up on a year ago. British exports to Singapore in the same period were worth £424 million, up 29 per cent on a year earlier. To take just one example, clothing exports are up 69 per cent to Singapore, 50 per cent to Hong Kong and 47 per cent to South Korea.

That is where many of the new jobs will come from. From businesses with the get up and go to find new markets, to design new products, to sell high value goods and services to the expanding economies of Asia. We must also ensure that British consumers can find British-made goods on the high street – goods made in the UK and at a price and quality to beat the imported product. We should have to make no apology for the home-made version. That is what competitiveness means. It is the only way to create and sustain jobs.

But, there is no magic potion.

First of all, we need to improve and improve our productivity so the value added in our economy grows. This will bring higher wages – linked to higher productivity, not higher inflation – and therefore higher living standards. Yes, John Monks is right, we have lost jobs in manufacturing. But we now have four million people producing more than seven million people produced just 15 years ago, and production has risen to record levels. But we need to do more.

Secondly, we must guard against the statutory imposition of unnecessary non-wage costs – which destroy jobs. That is why for example, I support consultation of workers – as good business – but object to the idea of statutory methods of enforcing it.

Thirdly, we need to nurture the smaller firms that will create the jobs of the future.

That is why we need sensible deregulation, enabling entrepreneurs to turn their enthusiasm into new jobs, without being strangled by red tape. That will take us closer to that elusive goal of full employment.

The jobs we need certainly won't come from panic measures to create jobs in the public sector. That would inevitably have to be paid for through higher taxes, or higher government borrowing. That would take spending power out of the hands of ordinary people and would quickly destroy jobs.

Action

Let me set out what I think needs to be done. All of us – trade unionists, employers, employees and Government – can work together to bring jobs, hope and opportunity to our people.

First, we must keep the right macro-economic framework in place. That requires a commitment from all of us to low and steady inflation and a stable economic environment.

Inflation is the enemy of employment, and inevitably strikes at the most vulnerable people in society. To keep inflation in check the Government must exercise a restrained monetary policy, but you too have a role, as Beveridge himself acknowledged:

> "*the primary responsibility of preventing a full employment policy from coming to grief in a vicious spiral of wages and prices will rest on those who conduct the bargaining on behalf of labour*".

This is the first action point – low inflation, and realistic pay bargaining. That is the way to get the low interest rates businesses want to invest and create new jobs.

Secondly, we must encourage enterprise and self-employment.

In the last 15 years the number of self-employed people has increased by 1.2 million. Between 1979 and 1991 900,000 new businesses were founded – most employing fewer than 20 people, at least in their early days. We must nurture and encourage these firms, and the men and women whose enterprise leads to their creation. Some will stay small. Fine. We need small businesses. We want corner shops. We want specialist manufacturers. We want the personal touch. Others though, will grow into larger businesses. The key point though is that all create jobs.

Thirdly, we must get a firm grip on the burden of regulation.

The most regulated economies are also those with the poorest records on job creation. The United States and Japan not only have fewer people out of work than most European countries; they also have more people in work. Only a handful of European countries can match their record of around 70 per cent of the population in work. Those countries – such as Denmark and the United Kingdom – are, as one would expect, also amongst the least regulated.

Supply side measures *do* work.

Of course, no one argues that we should abandon social protection. Some areas are non-negotiable. The United Kingdom has one of the best health and safety records in the world. It will stay that way. We also have some of the toughest anti-discrimination legislation – on both sex and race – and that will stay too.

What we must do, however, is strike a balance between the rights of those in work and the needs of those out of work. Extra social costs on jobs should not price others out of work.

We must strive to combine US-style job creation and enterprise with the kind of social standards we in Europe expect.

Fourthly, we must invest in our people.

Education and training are at the heart of our recent White Paper on Competitiveness.

People are the key to a successful economy: only if the elements of each individual are recognised and nurtured will we all achieve full potential.

There is common ground between us here.

Generations of relative neglect are being put right. Employers now spend over £20 billion a year on training. Since 1984, the number of working people receiving training has gone up by 70 per cent. We are reforming the system of vocational qualifications, and making rapid strides with the Investors in People Standard. 79 per cent of the workforce now have a recognised qualification. Almost one in three of our young people are entering higher education, a higher percentage than in France or Germany.

In 1979 – only 15 years ago – around 40 per cent of 16 year-olds stayed on in full-time education. Now 70 per cent stay on in education and in total 90 per cent of our 16 year-olds are in some form of education or training. But we must not stop there. That is why the White Paper announced that an extra £300 million will be spent on education and training, on top of the £1.25 billion for Modern Apprenticeships already announced in the Budget.

Fifthly, we must get those people who have lost their jobs back to work.

Fortunately, most people who lose their jobs find new employment in a relatively short time – half of all people made redundant find new jobs within three months. A small minority, however, about one in five – are still unemployed after a year or more.

There is a growing consensus that this is the group – the long-term unemployed – on which we must concentrate our attention, not least because so many of them are young people – often unskilled, usually male.

Much is already done to help them – over one and a half million opportunities costing £3 billion are available to help unemployed people this year. But there is also a growing consensus that new approaches may be required. I certainly have an open mind on this and always look seriously at any proposals aimed at getting people into work.

We may, for example, need to look at attitudes. Theirs and ours. Theirs, if young people are not willing to take advantage of what is on offer. Young men may, for example, have to consider whether jobs in the growing service sectors offer them better prospects than the blue collar jobs some still hanker after. Ours, if people are being denied jobs because of sex, colour or age.

Summary

These are my five *action points* for jobs:

- a stable economic environment, with low inflation;
- action to encourage self-employment and enterprise;
- a sensible balance between the rights of those in work and the needs of those out of work;
- a programme of investment in the skills and qualifications of our people;
- positive action to help unemployed people get back to work.

Much of this is already in place.

Inflation is, once again, under control. The message of deregulation is increasingly accepted. We were delighted, for example, when Chancellor Kohl proposed a Deregulation Task Force to look at the burden of EC legislation. And, of course, we in Government have accepted the CBI's targets for training and education.

If we are going to achieve all that, we will need a positive partnership in industry between employers and employees, to help British business to win. The right place for this partnership is the workplace; the last thing we need is a return to the bad old days of the 1960s and 1970s and failed corporatism.

There can be a positive role for trade unions – in the workplace, representing and selling their services to their members and helping companies to succeed. We have been enjoying the lowest level of strikes in this country since records began over a century ago. We have put harmony in place of strife – and we can build upon that. It is time for the trade union movement to come out of opposition by seeking partnership in the workplace and by cutting that discredited link with the Labour Party at a national level.

Unemployment is far too high and must come down further. How far and how fast will be determined not by targets but by the men and women in British industry making more and selling more. There can be a role for the trade unions in the battle against unemployment, but not a privileged one. Unemployed people here in the UK will look on amazed if we continue to fight old battles instead of working together in this great cause.

We all want to see more jobs and more opportunities for people. We already have one of the largest percentages of our working age population in work. We are also top of the European Premier League for growth this year, last year and we will be next year as well.

Our health and safety record is one of the best. Our production workers take home some of the highest rates of pay in Europe – OECD figures prove that.

The fall in our unemployment statistics demonstrates the success of the UK approach, with similar falls both in the numbers claiming unemployment benefits and of those unemployed under the Labour Force Survey, conducted in accordance with ILO rules. Economic indicators are moving in the right direction.

What matters most is that we all join together in facing up to the greatest economic policy issue of our time. Everyone in this country can make common cause. We must work together for jobs.

Questions to the speakers

Following their addresses to the conference, John Monks, Howard Davies and David Hunt briefly formed a panel to take a few questions from delegates.

John Evans of the Trade Union Advisory Committee of the OECD asked the panellists to comment on three points to emerge from the OECD *Jobs Study*. First, the recommendation that economies experiencing significant slack in their labour markets should expand demand. Secondly, the suggestion that trade unions had an important role to play in developing social consensus about how to handle technical change. And thirdly the fact that the OECD had made clear that high structural unemployment in Europe and working poverty in the US were problems of equal severity.

Both Howard Davies and David Hunt disputed whether the recommendation for an expansion of demand either referred to Britain or was suitable for Britain in the current phase of the economic cycle. Mr Davies felt that the balance of monetary and fiscal policy was roughly appropriate. Further reductions in interest rates would be unwise in present market conditions, and neither was there a case for additional public spending in aggregate (although, as Mr Davies had made clear in his presentation, there was a strong case for a shift in the *composition* of public spending toward investment). He agreed, however, that consensus over such issues as technical change was helpful and – reiterating the point made in his conference address – indicated that the problem of working poverty and widening earnings inequality would in due course almost certainly move higher up the policy agenda. Mr Davies and Mr Hunt both pointed to in-work benefits, such as Family Credit, as one means of alleviating working poverty.

David Hunt repeated his belief that consensus on such things as technical change would develop as a result of more social partnership at workplace level. But John Monks, while agreeing on the need for this, argued that there was also a need for social partnership at *national* level. A national social partnership, combined with a proper framework of regulation, could help the economy cope with structural change, assist competitiveness and lead to job creation. By way of example, Mr Monks pointed to health and safety as an area where Britain's record was relatively good. This demonstrated the importance of proper regulation, with the Health and Safety Commission and Executive demonstrating the value of widely respected national standard setting bodies.

Mike Barrett of the National League of Blind and Disabled reminded the conference of the 1944 Disabled Persons (Employment) Act the fiftieth anniversary of which was also being marked in 1994. Disabled people had not figured on the conference agenda despite the fact that disabled people have very high rates of unemployment. Mr Barrett commented that without wide ranging anti-discrimination legislation – akin to that operating in the US – any moves toward full employment might simply leave disabled people behind.

All three panellists agreed that the quota system for the employment of disabled people enshrined in the 1944 Act was not working well. Howard Davies looked to a dialogue between employers, government, unions and disabled people to consider a way forward. David Hunt said that the Employment Department's new Access to Work scheme – which compensates employers for the costs of employing disabled people under the scheme – would within the next year help the Employment Service meet its target for placing 55,000 unemployed people with disabilities into jobs. Mr Hunt also said, however, that he believed unfair discrimination against disabled people should be made illegal and supported a process of consultation on this matter. A consultation paper would soon be published. John Monks welcomed Mr Hunt's comment and highlighted the importance of providing equal access to disabled people.

Finally, Ms Lucy Daniels of Parents at Work asked the panellists if they felt that government, employers and trade unions could do more to encourage the sharing of available work which would not only help reduce unemployment but also help working parents.

Both David Hunt and Howard Davies felt that shorter working hours and family friendly working were to be encouraged if that was what people wanted but that this was best brought about by voluntary agreement between employers and employees rather than by regulation which could impose additional costs on employers. As Mr Davies pointed out, however, it was important for organisations like Parents at Work to keep pressing employers on this issue. Employers, said Mr Davies, often lacked imagination on how to re-organise work so a major task was required to change hearts and minds. John Monks broadly supported more family friendly working but added a note of caution. It was no good simply encouraging more part-time working, etc., if this meant that parents were unable to earn enough to support themselves and their children.

CHAPTER 4

A view from the opposition parties

JOHN PRESCOTT, MP,
Labour Party Spokesperson on Employment

ALEX CARLILE, QC, MP,
Liberal Democrat Spokesperson on Employment

JOHN PRESCOTT, MP,
Labour Party Spokesperson on Employment

The objective of full employment is now accepted by all. The 1994 White Paper stated that the primary aim and objective of government was the maintenance of a high and stable level of employment. I reminded people of that commitment in 1985 in my pamphlet *Planning for Full Employment.* At the time I was labelled a 'traditionalist' for talking about this even though there was mass unemployment.

Now I am amazed to find that, after 15 years of Tory government, David Hunt has accepted the objective of full employment – and not only that, he also says that full employment needs to be achieved by partnership.

Mass unemployment is back with us in the North, East, South and West as well as in many other countries. We all have to recognise that government can help create higher employment and affect the atmosphere – a word Mr Hunt uses – in which jobs are created. However, unlike Mr Hunt I don't accept that the deregulated model is anything to do with creating such an atmosphere for full employment.

The evidence is clear. 15 years of deregulation have only created unemployment. This government has never been interested in targeting jobs. They have targeted inflation, they have targeted interest rates and they have targeted growth. But employment and unemployment has simply been left to the market to determine.

The only time when the government shows concern over unemployment is when it begins to create a crisis for the public finances. My indictment of this government is that it has used unemployment as a tool of economic management. Unemployment has been used to discipline the labour force into a master–servant relationship; that is what Mr Hunt means by partnership with trade unions.

We have also had 15 years of fiddling the figures. If half the energy put into fiddling the figures had instead been put into getting people back to work we would probably have a lot more people at work.

Mr Hunt says that unemployment is down 310,000 over the past year. But the level of employment is also down, by 58,000. So where have all the unemployed gone? Not into jobs, but into the black hole of hidden unemployment. Into the desperate circumstances of our inner cities, and into the associated drug culture.

The Chancellor of the Exchequer, Mr Clarke, through his statements on how he expects the economy to grow, implicitly admits that official unemployment will stay at two and a half million to the next century. That will leave the real level at between four and five million.

Unemployment has been on a clear upward trend since the 1970s. The unemployment rate never rose above two per cent between the war and the 1970s. But the rate doubled in the 1970s and trebled again under the Tories in the 1980s and 1990s.

This upward trend is common to many countries although not to the same extent. The point we must realise – as Paul Ormerod shows in his paper for the conference (see Chapter 5) – is that even if we double the rate of economic growth to over four per cent per year we still won't achieve full employment in Britain. Growth alone, given the way employment is distributed at present by the market, will not create the levels of employment that we need.

All countries are affected by the same international economic forces but not all are affected as badly because they have different levels of government intervention and different social attitudes which combine to alter the market distribution of employment.

Japan, for example, uses a highly productive and competitive wealth creating manufacturing sector to sustain high levels of labour intensive employment in the service sector. Japan's is a culture in which it is considered better to maintain labour intensive and less efficient services rather than maintain mass unemployment. It is a culture in which sacking people is seen as a source of great shame, not a sign of toughness to be admired.

Scandinavia uses higher taxation to pay to maintain higher levels of employment in the public sector. This or the Japanese approach is not necessarily the right solution for Britain. But these examples prove that government *can* influence the level of employment – government *can* influence the culture and put full employment at the top of the agenda.

The conditions for full employment require a highly efficient, effective wealth creating industrial sector. To achieve this there is a need to use, in conjunction, macroeconomic policy, industrial policy, regional policy, training and education policy (including a training levy on employers) and a European policy (unlike the Government which has opted out of the European recovery programme).

All of these policies necessarily involve government. All are long-term. All involve creating the climate for job creation. But we can make a start in the short-term and the medium-term, and we can effect more immediate changes to policy to increase employment.

One thing I want to inject into the debate is the idea that there can be job targets. The TUC some time ago produced its plan for job targets. I have noticed that in the past few years the TUC has stopped doing this but targets seem relevant and perhaps the TUC should make them front stage again. After all, even the CBI must have implicit job targets in mind when from time to time it argues for more spending on infrastructure projects, etc. President Clinton set a target to create eight million jobs in four years – he has created three million already in 16 months, a good achievement even though Clinton is not satisfied with the quality of jobs being created.

The European Union – by way of the Delors White Paper's European Recovery Programme – has a target to create 15 million jobs by the end of the century. Britain's share of that would be to create one million jobs. Unlike the government I want to opt into that programme. I believe it is possible to create one million jobs during a single period of government.

If, however, politicians pluck a figure out of the air without working out where the jobs can come from or how they will be created, then they are in danger of being discredited. This is why I have proposed a Commission for Full Employment. If established this would define full employment, would establish a proper basis for measuring employment to replace the fiddles, would look at where the jobs will come from both short and long-term, would set realistic targets and would look at how to finance jobs programmes.

The Commission would consider some of the examples I have been suggesting for creating jobs, such as the following:

Public expenditure jobs audit: different mixtures of public expenditure will result in different levels of employment; employment must be a top priority in the assessment of expenditure decisions.

Different fiscal priority: people should not be taxed out of jobs because of government incompetence. In the North Sea, for example, the government has

65

decided to change Petroleum Revenue Tax to give more wells to the big oil companies thus discriminating against smaller companies that want to fill oil wells and create a demand for British manufacturing. The Treasury might think this is a good policy. But if policy makers are concerned about manufacturing and jobs they ought to have drawn a different conclusion.

Different investment criteria: I have, for example, proposed £509 million of first year investment allowances to treble the number of ships being built in Britain. This would create extra jobs and create demand for steel and related production.

New Treasury rules: there is a need to encourage more private sector investment in public projects covering such areas as transport, postal services and local authorities.

European finance: Britain could make far better use of the EU Development Funds and Investment and Infrastructure Funds. In addition more loans should be applied for from the European Investment Bank.

Regulated competition: take the bus industry. If this were regulated rather than made to conform to a competitive model, bus companies would be more able to plan and order new buses.

Local authority strategy: housing offers a prime example of what could be done. Local authorities have £5 billion of capital receipts from sales of council houses which they are not allowed to spend on new housing projects. If these resources were released, 120,000 homes could be provided for homeless people and 200,000 jobs would be created in the building industry, saving the Treasury almost £2 billion a year in benefit.

Social productivity: economic productivity dictates increasing output through reducing employment. Social productivity means increasing employment by creating jobs to improve the quality of public services. Provision of local services should be judged against social productivity as well as economic productivity. There is a need for more teachers, nurses and bus conductors and train guards, etc. It is much better to use tax revenues to improve such services and help unemployed people into jobs.

Energy conservation work: there is considerable scope to create real jobs in energy conservation that would improve energy efficiency in the home. This would also increase the disposable incomes of low income families enabling them to spend more in their local economies.

All these examples prove that there are many ways in which government can affect the level of employment. If we can achieve progress in such areas we can convince the electorate that government has a part to play in reducing unemployment and a responsibility to do so.

Moving beyond this to the second stage for achieving full employment will be far more difficult. Getting three to four million people back to work is not an easy proposition. But I believe it is not beyond possibility if we are prepared to give full employment political priority.

Full employment will require major social change. It will require all of us in the Labour movement to talk about what is a fair distribution of work and how we can all play a part in helping people get back to work. It will need a major and fundamental reform of the welfare state so that welfare acts as a bridge into work. More and more people are going to find that they will have to change jobs four or five times in their working lives – the whole welfare and National Insurance system will have to be adapted to cope with this.

Above all, full employment is going to require fundamental change in political thinking of the kind Keynes and Beveridge provided in the 1940s. We need the kind of commitment shown then – albeit in different circumstances. I believe it is possible to secure this. All we need is for full employment to become a political priority. This conference is a step in that direction.

ALEX CARLILE, QC, MP,
Liberal Democrats Spokesperson on Employment[1]

I am delighted that the TUC has with *Looking Forward to Full Employment* taken an initiative to cross party lines once again. There is no monopoly of wisdom on the issue of unemployment.

Both Paddy Ashdown and John Prescott have recently used the same sentence: "We must work for full employment if we are to unlock the country's potential". I am not going to accuse John Prescott of being a 'pro-Ashdownist' any more than I am going to accuse Paddy Ashdown of being a 'retro-socialist'. It is simply that they were both using common sense, a common sense that I hope we can maximise from this conference.

John Prescott also said that the government had made some misleading statements. I think that some they have not made are as misleading as some they have. For example, I doubt if David Hunt will have told you that the biggest increase in unemployment has been amongst the long-term male unemployed aged between 25–49. This has been a major increase that has undermined the economic and social fabric of the country.

Full employment in my view and the view of my party should be the aim. But like John Prescott we have to realise that full employment cannot be a promise based on the short-term.

For me, as a Liberal Democrat, full employment has intrinsic importance for the security of society. As one looks around one sees a deterioration of family life and a deterioration of the fabric of our cities. One sees an increase in mental illness. And I have seen over the past 25 years as a lawyer dealing with criminal cases, the sinister growth of a sub-economy dependent on drugs which sucks in young people – mainly young men – who are not able to earn a living from normal work. I think that is something to be deplored.

For all these reasons I welcome this debate on full employment. I sincerely hope though that we shall emerge not engrossed in the question some will want us to ask – namely, is full employment possible? – but enthused with new ideas on how to make full employment possible over a realistic time period.

We cannot pretend of course that the solution is simple. If our only answer to unemployment is to put skilled and talented people into low paid dead-end jobs, or put our young people onto courses that have no value other than as parking

---

[1] Mr Carlile's address was delivered during the conference panel session (see Chapter 5).

68

spaces away from the unemployment figures, then society will suffer as much as if those people were left languishing on the dole.

The starting point for job creation is sound macroeconomic policy. We must end once and for all the short-term approach to economic policy that has prevailed over the past three to four decades of boom and bust.

We must aim for greater industrial partnership and I believe the TUC's re-launch helps this. Partnership between employers, employees, trade unions and government is a fundamental ingredient of long-term economic prosperity.

We must, however, start with investment. Investment in effective and flexible training for a workforce that can adapt to an ever changing environment. And investment in the infrastructure. Everyone except the government is aware of the chronic state of many of the nation's schools and hospitals. Everyone except the government is aware of the shortage of decent housing and the need for a better transport infrastructure. And everyone – including, I suspect, the government though they may not admit it – is aware of the need for investment to revitalise our flagging manufacturing industry.

Some of this much needed investment would create new jobs in the public sector. But there are many things that can be achieved in the private sector to bring about a dramatic reduction in unemployment. Professor Layard (see Chapter 5) has some interesting ideas which are attractive in their very simplicity about the way in which one can move public spending from benefits to create jobs in the private sector in a very straightforward way. I think we have to recognise the outrageous cost of unemployment and then realise that it is possible to create jobs at no greater cost than keeping someone on benefit.

Turning to support for industry, in some respects the private sector has a great deal to answer for. Not the manufacturing sector but the financial markets, the bankers and venture capitalists. Go and ask a venture capitalist in Frankfurt to back a small business and what you will get is long-term involvement, non-executive involvement on the board, a month by month business plan scrutiny, and re-investment after two to three years to help the business grow. Ask the same of the British financial market and all you will get is a one off offer of help for a fat fee and the abandonment of the new business once the deal is set up. It seems to me that we will have to learn from some of the more successful employment and business creation techniques applied overseas if we are to achieve comparable success in the UK.

With sound economic policy and the necessary investment in skills and capital infrastructure, full employment is a realistic target. With a properly organised and motivated workforce where every individual is allowed to fulfil her or his potential, 'full employability', of which Paddy Ashdown has spoken, does become full employment and that is the order in which it happens.

Of course we have to recognise that we are talking about a political agenda here, one which will not always be popular and certainly not without cost. Hard decisions will have to be made if solid results are to be produced. But I hope that we will be able to look back on this conference in due course and see it as seminal in the process of building towards full employment.

CHAPTER 5

Full employment: key issues for the emerging debate

JOHN PHILPOTT, Director, Employment Policy Institute

While it is useful to look back to Beveridge and the 1944 White Paper to re-enlist the intellectual rigour and moral zeal enshrined in the post-war commitment to full employment, we must be forward looking in our search for solutions to the contemporary unemployment problem.

In advance of *Looking Forward to Full Employment*, the EPI therefore commissioned a set of detailed background papers from independent experts in the fields of economics, employment and public policy. The papers spanned virtually the entire range of issues that will need to be addressed if full employment is to be achieved (see Appendix B).

Three of the authors – Professor Richard Layard of the London School of Economics and Chair of the EPI's Research Committee, Ms Patricia Hewitt, outgoing Deputy Director of the Institute for Public Policy Research, and Professor Paul Ormerod, Chair of Full Employment UK – formed a panel for a discussion session at the conference. They were joined on the panel by Ms Kamlesh Bahl, Chair of the Equal Opportunities Commission, Mr Herman Ouseley, Chair of the Commission for Racial Equality and Mr Alex Carlile, QC, MP, of the Liberal Democrats.

This chapter provides a non-technical overview of the issues covered in the background papers and the various points made by panel members and delegates during the panel session.

Full employment and mass unemployment

In *Full Employment in a Free Society* Beveridge was more precise than the authors of the 1944 White Paper *Employment Policy*.[1, 2] The aim of policy should be 'full employment'. This meant an unemployment rate of three per cent or less of the workforce in a 'sellers market' in which the number of job vacancies outstripped the number of jobless men. Moreover, there should be no long-term unemployed. The margin of three per cent would *"consist of a shifting body of short-term unemployed who could be maintained without hardship by unemployment insurance"*.

Beveridge, in line with the White Paper, considered the prime responsibility for achieving this to rest with the state. The principal instrument would be demand management; as Keynes had shown, it was essential that the state should use the tools of financial policy to maintain an adequate level of demand for goods and services. Yet it would be wrong to conclude that this was considered all that was needed to achieve full employment.

The White Paper, for example, warned about the inflationary pressures that might be associated with the maintenance of a high and stable level of employment and contains extensive reference to what we would nowadays call 'supply side' measures as a way of mitigating them. Indeed, according to Nobel Laureate Professor James Meade – a key contributor to the White Paper – Keynes was concerned that inflationary pressures might build-up in the post-war economy if the unemployment rate were to fall much below eight per cent of the workforce.[3] Beveridge was also aware that the task of achieving full employment was far from straightforward and extended beyond demand management. He concluded his preface to *Full Employment in a Free Society* as follows:

"Unemployment cannot be conquered by a democracy until it is understood. Full productive employment in a free society is possible but it is not possible without taking pains. It cannot be won by waving a financial wand; it is a goal that can be reached only by conscious continuous organisation of all our productive resources under democratic control. To win full employment and keep it, we must will the end and must understand and will the means."

As events turned out, Beveridge's optimism that the means and the will could be marshalled to fight unemployment was vindicated throughout much of the post-war era. Full employment without serious inflation was maintained in conditions of excess demand for a generation after the war (although as Andrew Britton points out in his paper *Full Employment in a Market Economy* (see Chapter 2), this reflected a confluence of economic and social circumstances as much as any skill on the part of policy makers). Unfortunately, matters have deteriorated during the past twenty years. The UK economy nowadays 'overheats' at well in excess of three per cent unemployment. Over the last business cycle the unemployment rate averaged eight per cent – and long-term unemployment has re-emerged as a major social and economic problem (one in every three people currently unemployed have been without a job for at least a year). Few can be confident that the present recovery will on its own succeed where all those since the mid-1970s have failed and restore anything approaching full employment as envisaged by Beveridge.

The cost of this failure is truly immense. As David Piachaud outlines in his paper *A Price Worth Paying?* mass unemployment has bred poverty, damaged the health of individuals and whole communities and reduced social cohesion. It has also threatened to undermine the welfare state – the very existence of which was originally predicated by Beveridge on the assumption of full employment. The burden on the taxpayer of maintaining between two and three million people on the dole in 1994/1995 amounts to £26 billion or £9,000 per unemployed person. Piachaud calculates that if unemployment were reduced to its average level in the 1970s, the Exchequer cost would fall by the equivalent of 10 pence on the basic rate of income tax.

This of course is a big if. Yet Piachaud is surely right to conclude that mass unemployment should not be passively accepted as a *fait accompli*. As he concludes, *"Britain has a choice"*. The initial task facing those who still aspire to full employment, however, is, as Andrew Britton remarks, to convince people in the 1990s that full employment is more than just a political slogan borrowed from the past – and make clear the requirements, and costs, associated with a strategy to achieve it.

More than just a slogan?

If the opinion polls are to be believed most people in Britain today remain unconvinced that full employment can be achieved. This is unsurprising. One needs to be well over the age of majority to have any real memory of a time when finding a job was relatively easy. Nowadays few people feel fully secure in their employment and the common belief is that never again will there be sufficient jobs "to go round" even during good times for the economy. In addition to pessimism, many are also confused by the language of full employment. It often conveys an impression of full-time male employees working flat-out, which can seem outdated in the 1990s when women make up half the work-force and more people work part-time or are self-employed.

Jill Rubery in her background paper *What Do Women Want from Full Employment?* is critical of the "gender blindness" evident in definitions of full employment and unemployment. Both Rubery and Patricia Hewitt in her paper *Full Employment for Men and Women* agree that full employment must mean employment for both women and men. As Hewitt makes clear, however, while this will mean re-evaluating the assumptions surrounding Beveridge's definition of full employment the goal itself is still appropriate today. In other words, although the changed nature of the labour market in the 1990s has major implications for the *policies* society will have to adopt to achieve full employment, the goal as set out by Beveridge remains valid.

If, for example, the demand for labour could once again be sustained at the level required to meet Beveridge's full employment target, modern day social preference – as mitigated by prevailing tax and benefit systems – would undoubtedly result in a very different pattern of employment (in terms of the mix of male and female and full-time and part-time workers, etc.) than that which prevailed under full employment in the post-war era. But we should not (as the growing number of 'future of work' gurus often do) confuse discussion of how society should respond to a changing *pattern* of employment with the issue of how to expand the *volume* of employment.

Common pessimism about the prospects for full employment would of course be justified if it were impossible to expand the volume of employment. If there were only a fixed amount of work to be done policy-makers would be virtually impotent in the face of, say, new technology or an increase in the number of people looking for jobs. At best all that could be hoped for would be to share the available work around. But in a world of mass desire, not to mention poverty and need, the belief that there can never again be jobs for all who seek them seems hard to sustain. The problem of mass unemployment instead lies in society's inability to maintain demand in the economy at a rate sufficient to absorb idle hands without stoking up inflation (and creating balance of payments problems). In order to translate full employment from a slogan into a set of practical propositions we must therefore – as Beveridge would certainly have appreciated – understand why so much unemployment is nowadays required to keep inflation in check.

'Core unemployment'

The crux of the post-war remedy for unemployment was to dampen fluctuations in the economic cycle in order to ensure that there was no prolonged deficiency in demand of the kind experienced during the inter-war years. Since the mid-1970s, however, although unemployment still rises and falls broadly in line with fluctuations in demand and output, increasing emphasis has tended to be placed upon the 'core' of unemployment around which fluctuations in the cycle occur. This has been especially true in Britain and most of the countries of the European Union. The EU countries as a whole have experienced a trend increase in the core rate of unemployment to around 10 per cent of the workforce. In the United States, by contrast, unemployment has fluctuated around a core rate of six to seven per cent – now considerably lower than the EU average, having generally been higher in the 1950s and 1960s – while Japan has maintained both a low core unemployment rate of roughly two per cent and also prevented significant fluctuations of unemployment.

'Core' unemployment is a less loaded term than the more commonly used term 'structural' unemployment. For some, structural unemployment means a mismatch between the skills or location of jobless people and the skill requirements and location of job vacancies. For others, it implies so-called 'inflexibility' in institutional arrangements that make the labour market more 'rigid' or more prone to inflation at any given level of demand for labour. In particular the term often implies that only supply side measures are appropriate for dealing with the problem. In general, this is probably a valid implication. But some economists would argue that measures operating on the demand as well as the supply side of the economy would have a role to play in combating core unemployment as part of a strategy for full employment. It is preferable to have an open mind on all of these issues so we shall stick with the term core unemployment – as Andrew Britton remarks in his paper, unemployment is not a simple problem with one explanation and one cure.

The initial onset of the rise in the core unemployment problem in Britain as elsewhere is generally felt to be associated with the various economic 'shocks' of the 1970s and early 1980s – notably the sharp oil price hikes – and over the longer-term 'strains' caused by structural change which have led to job losses in traditional industries and in particular caused a reduction in the demand for unskilled workers.

Some explanations of the rising core point to interactions between periodic bouts of deficient demand and a deterioration in the strength of the supply side of the economy. The loss of industrial capacity and skills, combined with the creation of a large group of long-term unemployed who are not easily re-absorbed into jobs even during periods of economic recovery, weakens an economy's capacity to reduce unemployment substantially without a resurgence of inflation.

A related, albeit even more fundamental issue for Britain, is raised by Christine Greenhalgh and Mary Gregory in their background paper *Why Manufacturing Still Matters*. They point to 'de-industrialisation' leading to substantial job losses in manufacturing as a major cause not only of unemployment in Britain but also of the nation's general economic difficulties. Greenhalgh and Gregory show that over the period 1960–90 – and especially since 1979 – Britain has shed manufacturing jobs at a far faster rate than any of the G5 major industrial nations.

This outcome could of course be viewed as a sign of success because manufacturing productivity has risen sharply. Improved productivity should serve as a boost to domestic output and, by increasing competitiveness in world markets, also assist export-led growth. This can generate sufficient prosperity to underpin job creation in the service sector if not manufacturing itself. However, as Greenhalgh and Gregory show, Britain's de-industrialisation has corresponded with a loss of market share in both domestic and export markets for manufactured goods, while the growth in manufacturing output has been weaker than that of any other G5 nation.

The central issue here, as far as core unemployment is concerned, is not that jobs are being lost from manufacturing – this will tend to occur come what may because new technology is continually providing scope for improvements in productivity. The issue is rather that of the consequences of the apparent lack of competitiveness of Britain's manufacturing sector.

Poor manufacturing performance makes it more difficult for Britain to maintain a healthy balance of trade and limits the scope for generating a sustained reduction in unemployment. For one thing, policy makers will be reluctant to boost demand for goods and services for fear that balance of payments problems might lead to downward pressure on the pound and – because this would result in higher import prices in the shops – upward pressure on inflation. Moreover, Greenhalgh and Gregory point out that manufacturing sustains a far higher proportion of jobs throughout the economy than is measured by its share in total employment because it makes substantial purchases from the service sector. A weak manufacturing sector is therefore likely to result in a lower overall level of employment.

Globalisation and new technology

A common explanation for the rise in core unemployment is an observed shift in the demand for labour favouring those with skills as against those without skills. At present in Britain, for example, despite the fact that unemployment rates at all levels of skill are high as a hangover from the recession, rates for unskilled workers are five times as high as those for better skilled workers.[4] Perhaps even more significant, the unskilled at present comprise half of Britain's one million long-term unemployed, while many more unskilled people have left the workforce altogether. Roughly a third of unskilled men of working age are 'non-employed', i.e. either unemployed or existing outside the labour market.[5]

Chris Freeman's paper *Technical Change and Unemployment* examines the role of technology in causing this shift. He focuses in particular on the dramatic impact of information and communications technology (ICT) which – like steam power or electrification in previous eras – represents a quantum leap in the prevailing mode of technology affecting not just a few products or services but *every* industry and *every* service. This change in the technological mode benefits most those workers skilled enough to perform higher level jobs, especially jobs requiring significant 'brain power' in order to fulfil so-called 'problem solving' tasks. It causes difficulty, however, for those equipped only for traditional routine forms of work based on either simple 'muscle power' or the ability to operate within a fairly standard production line or service function setting. Opportunities for the unskilled and less skilled are thus diminishing, an outcome that is putting downward pressure on pay at the bottom end of the labour market and making it more likely that unskilled workers will lose their jobs (or be unable to find new ones).

Some economists, however, while not disputing the importance of technology also argue that increased competition from low cost developing countries – arising from the ever more 'globalised' pattern of investment, production and trade – has also been a major factor underlying the fall in demand for unskilled workers in developed economies. In his paper, *Does Globalisation Threaten Low Skill Western Workers?*, Richard Freeman therefore reviews the case for and against this trade effect on the labour market.

Economists' theories of international trade – which predict that in order to maximise the gains from trade a country will exploit its comparative advantage in available resources – suggests that the effect of globalised trade on the labour market prospects of low skilled workers could be considerable. The developed economies are relatively more abundant in skilled workers so it makes sense for them to specialise in goods and services with a high skill content and rely on imports of less skill intensive products from developing countries. As more cheap imports have become available, it is therefore argued, the general tendency of western economies has thus been to shift even more in the direction of higher skill labour, reducing opportunities for the unskilled. Some economists suggest that just such a trade effect has led to a 20 per cent fall in demand for unskilled labour in the developed economies during the past 30 years.[6]

Richard Freeman is agnostic. While concluding that globalisation has, and probably will have, a much greater impact on unskilled labour in the West than many economists have thus far estimated, he questions whether the effect has been as dramatic as some claim. One reason is simply that developed economies mostly trade amongst themselves, using broadly similar proportions of skilled and unskilled workers (according to the OECD *Jobs Study*[7] exports from 'low wage countries' account for only 1.5 per cent of total expenditure on goods and services by the developed economies). Another reason is that the impact of globalisation falls on the tradable sector (primarily manufacturing) which in most developed economies accounts for a relatively small share of total employment. Since unskilled workers are under pressure throughout the labour market, the likelihood therefore is that their prospects are on the whole affected by technology more than by trade.

The importance of being adaptable

The preceding discussion should not of course be taken to imply that trade and technology are things to be avoided. On the contrary, they are to be encouraged. By raising productivity, technological change helps lower costs and prices and enables people to buy more goods and services. Moreover, technology generates new investment, new forms of employment and new products – the demand for which, along with that for existing products, is boosted by the higher real pay afforded by improved productivity. Similarly, competition inspired by free trade benefits consumers in the form of lower prices while at the same time opening up new export markets. So trade agreements, such as the General Agreement on Tariffs and Trade (GATT) should be supported.

However, while most of society stands to gain from these processes there will be losers if labour markets and related institutions fail to adapt to change. If the number of losers is simply allowed to rise, both they and other potential losers will become fearful of, and hostile to, change. Such hostility stands in the way of economic and social progress. Even more worryingly, it can give rise to political tensions that undermine the very foundations of democratic society. 'Adaptability' must therefore become the *sine qua non* of economic and employment policy.

Significantly, adaptability is the key theme of the recent OECD *Jobs Study*. The study concludes that the way societies adapt to shocks and strains is what in the end matters for employment and unemployment, not the shocks and strains themselves. All the developed economies are affected by change in much the same way but some have fared better than others. Yet the OECD is careful not to single out any particular 'model' of adaptability since almost nowhere have labour markets adapted satisfactorily to change. The OECD prefers instead to offer some policy options, based on multi-country experience, in the hope that countries will choose paths away from mass unemployment that both create jobs and maintain social cohesion.

The need for a 'middle way'

What sort of 'model' of adaptability would best suit Britain? It is often said that a choice has to be made between a de-regulated/minimal welfare US-style model and a 'European Union' model comprising a more regulated labour market and generous welfare provision. In tabloid terms, the former model is said to be friendly to job creation, the latter a recipe for unemployment. This is something of a caricature. The EU after all is not a homogeneous entity and it is arguable that some 'social market' EU states, notably Germany, have performed better in terms of unemployment and adapting to change than the more 'free market' US.[8] The tabloid caricature nonetheless bears some resemblance to reality.

According to the OECD, the European Union has since the mid-1970s, maintained strong productivity growth through shedding workers from traditional sectors but, with the exception of some increase in public sector employment, generated few new jobs. The result has been high unemployment and particularly long-term unemployment – half those unemployed in the EU have been without employment for more than a year.

The US economy by contrast, although growing at a comparable rate, has been better at creating jobs – both high and low skilled – mostly in the private services sector. But productivity has grown only slowly and there have been profound implications for pay. Wage differentials have widened dramatically. Richard Freeman *op.cit.* notes that a man in the bottom tenth of the hourly earnings distribution in the US earns just over a third as much as the average (i.e. median) man. In Europe, by contrast, a similarly placed man earns two thirds of the average. However, the problem in the US is not merely one of more unequal earnings – absolute poverty amongst the working poor has also grown to staggering proportions. Freeman calculates that even an unemployed man in an advanced European country now has a far higher living standard than a man working full-time situated toward the bottom of the US pay league.

This outcome partly reflects developments in trade and technology of the kind we have already discussed. But as Paul Ormerod points out in his paper, *Can Economics Solve the Problem of Unemployment?* the US job creation record and the associated depression of wages is also to a large extent explained by a large influx of migrant labour from Mexico prepared to work for poverty pay. An indirect consequence of this has been increased 'non-employment' and rising crime; to avoid low paid jobs many unskilled Americans have opted out of the legitimate labour market altogether.[9]

The UK has spent the last 15 years moving in the direction of the US-model while attempting to maintain something resembling a European style welfare state. Kenneth Clarke's recent Mais Lecture[10] – in which the Chancellor of the Exchequer stated that unemployment must become the *"main preoccupation"* of policy makers in the 1990s – indicates that he believes such a 'hybrid' model offers a means of securing full employment without creating a class of working poor. Yet as Chris Pond argues in his paper *Building Full Employment Without*

Low Pay, earnings have become more unequal in Britain and the numbers in poverty have also risen (albeit as yet to nothing like the same extent as in the US).

Neither has the pay off in terms of jobs in Britain been anything like as strong as in the US. And most new jobs created in Britain in the 1980s and during the course of the present recovery have been part-time and taken by women entering the labour market. Unskilled males (and also to some extent more skilled former manual workers whose skills have been made redundant in the course of structural change) have tended to remain without jobs existing on one form of meagre welfare benefit or another. Some are visible and 'officially' long-term unemployed on Income Support, others 'non-employed' and in receipt of sickness related benefits. The perversity of the benefits system (for reasons we shall discuss in more detail later) has also meant that many of these jobless men have been joined on welfare by their female partners.

Britain's hybrid 'work and welfare' model therefore seems to have created the worst of both worlds – more relatively poor people in work but also a high level of unemployment and welfare dependency. One option would be to reject the hybrid model in favour of a full-blown de-regulated model and cut welfare to the bone. Those tempted to take this course, however, ought to listen to what the Americans are saying about a simplistic de-regulated approach: "been there, don't like it, want something better".

The present US Government is seeking to establish a new model – one that aims to create not just more jobs but also 'good' (i.e. skilled, well paid, 'problem solving') jobs while at the same time supporting the incomes in work of those with low skills who can command only a low market wage. This 'middle way' approach is the brainchild of US Labor Secretary Robert Reich and was high-lighted at the G7 'Jobs Summit'. The EU too, as the Delors White Paper has shown, is also looking for a middle way that will create jobs and preserve social solidarity. Britain should be flowing with this tide by developing its own progressive 'middle way' within the context of a strategy for full employment.

Key policy issues

From the conference papers and other available material it is possible to distil some policy ideas which, if knitted together, could form individual elements of a strategy for full employment. Here, rather than outline a specific strategy, we shall simply consider some of the key underlying policy issues as drawn from the conference papers. These are: labour market regulation; equal opportunities; skills and competitiveness; employment taxes and benefit reform; active labour market policies; the role of the public sector and 'social employment'; macroeconomic issues; and pay and productivity. We shall then conclude by examining whether there is a need to set a target for the reduction in unemployment.

Labour market regulation
The case for a de-regulated labour market rests on the belief that regulation – in very broad terms employment protection and minimum wage legislation, plus adequate legal backing for trade unions – renders markets less flexible and less adaptable. David Marsden in his paper *Regulation vs. De-regulation: Which Way for Europe's Labour Market?* questions this assumption.[11] Part of the problem is that the labour market is far from homogeneous. While regulation might harm employment prospects in some corners of the market – principally the low productivity end – it can enhance matters in those segments where what Marsden calls 'co-operative exchange' is important for creating productivity enhancing relations between employers and workers.

This helps explain the equivocation of the OECD's *Jobs Study* on the subject of employment protection legislation. The OECD finds that while such legislation preserves jobs it also deters employers from hiring because of the costs of shedding labour. But it also finds that by encouraging long-term relationships between employers and workers employment protection can increase the volume of on-the-job training in the economy. In terms of Marsden's analysis, crude de-regulation right across the labour market may indeed boost low wage low productivity jobs. But such a move can be counter-productive if what one wants is a high skill economy. Chris Pond's paper makes a similar point in relation to minimum wage legislation.

Marsden goes on to point out more generally that measures such as formal consultation procedures of the kind common in Germany, enhance 'co-operative exchange' between workers and employers and thus make labour markets much more flexible and adaptable than is the case in the low trust insecure environment of what might best be describe as a 'hire and fire' culture. Others observing this situation have concluded that the statutory imposition of consultation procedures on large European companies – as proposed under the Social Chapter of the Maastricht Treaty but opposed by the UK government and many employers – should thus be seen as a development to be embraced.[12] More generally, however, Marsden implies that constructive dialogue between the social partners is ultimately more important than EU legislation.

The conclusion to be drawn from this is not that all regulation is good and all de-regulation is bad. The secret is to find the right balance of intervention within a progressive policy of re-regulation. This balance should seek to ensure that low productivity jobs are not needlessly destroyed (or their creation wantonly prevented). But at the same time re-regulation should be used to gear the economy to compete at the high productivity end of world markets where Britain's comparative advantage surely lies.

Equal opportunities
As Jill Rubery and Patricia Hewitt discuss (the latter at the conference as well as in her paper), appropriate re-regulation – backed up by other measures such as better child care to help all mothers but especially jobless lone parents – would help to foster equal opportunities. Britain's army of part-time women workers – almost half of all women in employment work part-time compared with fewer than 10 per cent of men – have come to represent the archetypal 'flexible' workforce but most have fewer rights than full-timers under British labour law. Women are also those most affected by the abolition of the Wages Councils.

Kamlesh Bahl of the Equal Opportunities Commission developed this issue in her contribution to the panel session and argued that it was vital to challenge the usual assumptions about the role of women in the jobs market (a point re-inforced during the discussion by Ms Shelagh Diplock of The Fawcett Society). In particular, Bahl questioned the assumption that women freely choose part-time work in preference to full (or fuller) time work.

Policy makers should, according to Bahl, pose three questions when considering how to improve the lot of women in the labour market. First, would women work more hours if their partners were not working such long hours and could share in child care? Secondly, would single mothers or the partners of unemployed or low income men in receipt of benefit work longer hours if this did not adversely affect their benefits position (see also the section on benefit below)? And thirdly, would the pattern of women's work be different if they were able to secure affordable and quality child care?

If the issues underlying these questions were addressed, Bahl argued, the problem of women being segregated into low-paid jobs with fewer employment rights would be much reduced. In particular, it is important that part-time jobs – often at present with reduced training opportunities – do not simply become a 'dead end' for women workers, i.e. full employment for women must mean more than simply jobs at any price.

The matter of employment rights for part-timers may be set to change following the recent ruling on this matter by the Law Lords. The full implications of the ruling – which, following a legal challenge brought against the government by the Equal Opportunities Commission, found the UK to be in breach of European law on equal opportunities – are at the time of writing as yet unclear.

Hewitt argues the more general point, however, that Britain should adopt the principle of 'equal treatment' of part-time employees on a pro-rata basis with full-timers. She considers this essential to a new system of 'fair flexibility' in working time. This, Hewitt argues, could form part of a strategy for reducing unemployment and at the same time improve the quality of work and family life for both women *and* men. Hewitt believes that reform of working time would also enhance efficiency, a point backed-up by Chris Freeman *op.cit.* who points out that the new mode of technology centred on information and communications technology is geared toward flexible forms of working. Regulations and benefit systems based upon traditional forms of working will thus hamper the ability of economies to adapt to change.

In this context Herman Ouseley of the Commission for Racial Equality provided the conference with a timely reminder that equal opportunities also means offering a fair deal in the labour market to people from ethnic minorities. The issue of racial discrimination in the labour market was not covered explicitly in the conference papers (for a clear analysis see Brown's 1990 report for the EPI on this subject).[13] Ouseley pointed out that even in the halcyon days of full employment in the 1960s young blacks experienced mass unemployment. It was therefore important to avoid marginalising people from ethnic minorities – especially those in the more deprived parts of Britain's inner cities – when attempting to move forward to full employment in the 1990s.

Differential unemployment rates between whites and ethnic minorities – which had narrowed in the late 1980s – have widened again in the 1990s. According to Ouseley, it would appear that some employers used what amounts to a discriminatory form of 'last in first out' approach to lay-offs during the recession. Unemployment rates for most ethnic minority groups are currently two to three times higher than the average for white people – and the problem is even worse amongst young people.

Ouseley thus argued that remedies for discrimination, and greater emphasis on racial equality designed to foster fairness and justice and aid social cohesion, would have to be central to any practical solution to unemployment. A policy for full employment would thus have to be accompanied by a policy for full equal opportunities – something the trade unions would have an important role in helping to secure. Ouseley outlined four key action points: equal access to training opportunities; recognition of the skills and experience of people from ethnic minorities; positive action on under-representation of ethnic minorities in employment however this manifested itself; and a Racial Equality Standard so that the claim of being an 'equal opportunities employer' would gain real meaning.

Skills and competitiveness

As Chris Freeman's paper cited earlier makes clear, the adjustment needed to create a high skill economy will involve improvements in education and training and related measures to assist the diffusion of information and computer technology. He advocates in particular substantial investment in 'information highways and by-ways' based upon digital technology. Such investment plays an important part in the Clinton administration's plan for economic prosperity in the US, and – along with trans-European transport and energy networks – is a dominant theme in the Delors White Paper's competitiveness programme.

A highly skilled workforce will be crucial to exploiting the opportunities such technology offers for creating new markets and jobs. Everybody, of course, is in favour of education and training. Most people, for example, have welcomed the government's Modern Apprenticeship programme outlined in the recent 'Competitiveness' White Paper;[14] it is vital that we stop producing wave after wave of young people too unskilled to hold down a properly-paid job in a modern economy. Similarly, 'Life-long learning' and training for the unemployed are also seen as ways of preventing skills 'mismatches' of the kind that cause inflation to emerge even when unemployment is high. But as Ewart Keep and Ken Mayhew point out in a paper prepared prior to the conference and supplied to delegates, the assertion that more skills are needed is in itself vacuous. It is also necessary to ensure that the provision of skills is matched by the capacity and willingness of companies to use them. If not, costly investment could be wasted.

Keep and Mayhew argue that while a proportion of British employers are already taking the high quality route to international competitiveness, too many remain wedded to low quality products because high quality strategies require substantial investment and radical changes in corporate organisation. The underlying problem is the short-termism that bedevils so much of British industry – the quest for quick profits and dividends takes precedence over long-term planning and investment.

It might, ironically, be argued that this failure to make use of skills is good news for unskilled workers since it stems the shift in demand away from unskilled and toward skilled labour. The flaw in this argument, however, as Greenhalgh and Gregory's findings discussed earlier show, is that Britain's manufacturers have over time been losing out in world and domestic markets and manufacturing output has grown relatively sluggishly. So unskilled jobs are being lost notwithstanding the reluctance of many companies to move upmarket. Simply accepting the low quality scenario will only make matters worse. While it is tempting to argue that things can be improved if companies are able to become more competitive (through currency devaluation or by reducing the cost of employing unskilled labour) this can be no more than a palliative. If British companies are to survive long-term they will have to upgrade the quality of their products.

Unfortunately, this leaves policy-makers with a problem. It is far from easy in a free market economy to persuade companies to behave differently. Exhortation through the Training and Enterprise Councils (TECs) may persuade more employers to become 'Investors in People' or participate in similar initiatives – but many employers still present a deaf ear. The OECD *Jobs Study* considers the alternative of a training levy – recently recommended by the House of Commons Trade and Industry Committee[15] – an option which is worthy of further consideration. But it may be the case anyway that the emphasis on training or skills *per se* is misguided.

Keep and Mayhew, for example, believe that more should be done in the first instance to encourage companies to think strategically – if they do this they are more likely to operate in ways designed to make use of skills. Whether this is a job for TECs is a moot point – perhaps the joint TECs/Chamber of Commerce model which some prefer offers a better institutional mechanism for promoting such change. Keep and Mayhew, citing the work of other economists, also indicate that full-time education, rather than training, will assume increasing prominence as a way of altering the behaviour of companies.

There has already been a sudden expansion in the numbers of young people staying on at school or moving into further and higher education before entering the labour market (which may represent a supply side response to the shift in demand away from unskilled labour). This supply side trend, it is argued, may so alter the incentives facing employers that many more will choose to adopt a high quality product strategy. Keep and Mayhew remain sceptical.

The conclusion to be drawn from this discussion is that one should be wary of arguments for full employment that blithely refer to the importance of education and training. A policy for skills must be wedded to a full blown competitiveness package and industrial strategy. Greenhalgh and Gregory indicate that measures to enhance innovation and encourage ever greater use of technology as well as skills would have to be key components of a policy to re-build Britain's manufacturing base. This view is re-inforced by a recent analysis of British economic performance by a group of economists formerly employed at the now defunct National Economic Development Office (NEDO). This analysis highlights the need for wholesale institutional change in order to promote more effective financing and organisation of British industry.[16]

The government's recent 'Competitiveness' White Paper shows some recognition of the need for change but appears reluctant to admit to past policy failures and offers little in the way of additional resources. Irrespective of this, however, it is important to bear in mind that even if a competitiveness package were to succeed in creating more and better jobs the improvement would take some time, perhaps a generation, to fully emerge. Clearly, therefore, any strategy for full employment will also have to incorporate measures with a shorter pay off time – and offer hope and opportunity to those whose natural capacity to learn may prevent them from ever obtaining high skilled 'problem solving' jobs.

Employment taxes and benefits reform
The choices which employers and individuals make in the labour market are influenced by the tax and benefit system. Some taxes, for example employers' National Insurance contributions (NICs), directly raise the cost of labour over and above the amount employers have to pay out in wages to employees. This may affect the willingness of employers to hire labour, especially low productivity workers. Such taxes also influence the pattern and structure of employment and unemployment as well as the overall demand for labour. For example, British employers at present pay no contributions on earnings of less than £56 per week – which acts as an implicit 'subsidy' to hire part-time workers. Such jobs may be acceptable to women who wish to combine employment with child care responsibilities but may not attract unskilled male 'breadwinners' who seek full-time jobs. The rules governing employers' NICs therefore play a part in tilting the structure of employment in favour of part-time women workers.

It is sometimes suggested that such taxes on labour should be substantially reduced to boost employment opportunities. Andrew Britton therefore considers whether large scale adjustment of taxes of this kind might play a role in a full employment strategy. An obvious difficulty is loss of tax revenue to the Exchequer. This would be partly offset by savings in benefit as a consequence of lower unemployment, but Britton nonetheless expects the net cost having accounted for this to be considerable. Assuming these revenue losses have to be made up (to avoid cuts in public spending or higher borrowing) additional income tax or VAT would have to be raised.

This, of course, would be unpalatable for taxpayers – so some people argue instead that any compensatory revenue should be raised by taxing so-called 'anti-social activities', for example, the pollution which many companies cause as a by-product of their production processes. This seems attractive. It would meet 'Green' objectives in the process of helping the jobless. But desirable though such a tax shift would be it does not guarantee a 'free lunch'. The likelihood is that pollution taxes would in full or in part be passed on to consumers in the form of higher prices. Therefore, whether imposed on the consumer or the taxpayer, there would ultimately be some price to pay if policy makers sought to create more jobs by slashing employers' NICs. Much then depends upon whether taxpayers (or consumers) consider the price worth paying. This of course is a matter of social choice as much as of economics. It is worth noting, however, that cutting tax contributions paid by employers on people they *already* employ would represent a deadweight loss to the Exchequer. When this loss is accounted for the net cost of each *extra* job created by such a tax cut often turns out to be much higher than that associated with an alternative job creating use of the same amount of revenue.

The provision of benefits also affects the labour market. If the benefits system did not exist it is likely that there would be more low paid employment. But the consequence would be mass poverty (and, in all likelihood, a still higher rate of crime as more people sought higher earnings from illegal activities, such as drug pushing). Nobody wants this in Britain, but neither do we want people to remain unemployed. The key issue, therefore, is to make the benefit system more 'job friendly' without punishing those who comprise the poorest and most disadvantaged sections of the population.

Some advocate 'in-work' supplements (such as the means tested 'Family Credit') to the earnings of people who take low paid jobs in order to help them off Income Support. A fundamental problem with this approach is that the supplements are income related and give rise to the so-called 'poverty trap', i.e. recipients of in-work supplements find that they are little better off if they try to raise their earnings because of the withdrawal of the supplement. Practical problems can also arise as a result of the bureaucracy involved in the administration of the benefits system.

Family Credit, for example, is not payable until a person has been employed for a period often lasting several weeks (so that the details of the job can be processed) whereas Income Support ceases to be paid as soon as an unemployed person enters work. The prospect of hardship during the interim period before moving onto Family Credit – not to mention the uncertainty surrounding the fact that the claim for the Credit might be turned down – may deter an unemployed person from giving up the meagre 'security' offered by Income Support. It may therefore be necessary to provide some form of 'bridging payment' or lump-sum 'Back to Work' payment of the kind provided to unemployed people by the Employment Service in certain areas of Britain. Further disincentives can also arise if, as is often the case nowadays, the low-paid jobs on offer are themselves relatively insecure. It takes time to process new claims for Income Support – unemployed people may therefore be reluctant to take a low-paid job, irrespective of the availability of Family Credit, because they fear that if the job were to quickly disappear it would be difficult to 'sign back-on' for unemployment related benefit.[17]

Hewitt emphasises the importance of the changing pattern of employment in this respect. She argues that many families find themselves trapped between a so-called 'flexible' labour market creating more part-time and temporary jobs and a benefit system still geared to the post-war ('Beveridge-style') labour market where most jobs were full-time and largely taken by men.

Both Hewitt and Rubery *op.cit.* highlight the particular problems this causes for women. Means tested benefits (whether Income Support or Family Credit) are assessed on the basis of family incomes – the partners of unemployed men may therefore find that they will reduce the overall family income if they take a job offering less than sufficient to 'float' the family off benefit completely. Since most jobs being taken by women at present are part-time and relatively poorly paid this effectively shuts the women partners of unemployed men (or those receiving 'in-work' benefits) out of the labour market altogether. A worrying side effect of this is a polarisation in society between 'job rich' families where both partners work and 'job poor' families where neither partner works – the wife of an unemployed man is two to three times less likely to be in employment than the wife of a man in work.

Some suggest that a so-called Citizen's Income could help overcome many of the problems associated with means tested benefits. Citizens' Income would in effect act like a universal 'benefit' that every person in society would be entitled to as of right irrespective of what they earn. People could use this to supplement earnings but it would not vary with earnings or depend upon whether a person was employed or unemployed. Unfortunately, if provided at a reasonable level this would almost certainly prove to be very expensive – company profits or individual incomes would have to be taxed quite heavily to pay for it. A prerequisite of a Citizens' Income would thus seem to be some acceptance on the part of the 'haves' that the 'have nots' should be provided with an equal stake in society. This is a laudable aspiration but cannot simply be taken for granted.

Another alternative would be to provide more 'flexibility' within the Income Support system enabling unemployed people to work in temporary jobs for a small amount of money without losing benefit (in effect, extending the current system of earnings disregards). This idea is in some ways attractive, although it would run the risk of creating a class of 'odd-jobbers' constantly part-dependent on the state for income. In particular, it might create problems for the Employment Service since it could open up considerable scope for benefit fraud. Such a reform can nonetheless be recommended although it should really be seen as a palliative designed to cope with a labour market characterised by job scarcity and insecure forms of work, rather than something that would play a major role in any fully fledged strategy for full employment.

Finally, it is worth mentioning a problem common to any form of benefit top-up to wages (whether universal or means tested), i.e. it can act as an incentive for employers to cut pay rates in the knowledge that the taxpayer will pick up the tab. This too would raise the tax burden – and might end up subsidising the worst kind of inefficient exploitative employer (although such an effect could be mitigated by a sensibly applied form of minimum pay legislation).

Active labour market policies
The above discussion might be taken to imply that the main problem with the benefit system is that people on benefit are caught in the 'unemployment trap' and are worse off if they take a job. This may be true for some groups such as single parents and unemployed men with large numbers of dependants. But as Piachaud *op.cit.* shows most unemployed people are far worse off out of work – this is why poverty has increased so dramatically as unemployment has risen since the 1970s, and is a fact that demolishes the myth that the unemployed are 'workshy'. The most fundamental problem with the benefit system therefore, as Richard Layard argues in his paper *Preventing Long-Term Unemployment in Europe*, is simply that people are allowed to stay on benefit for too long without being given adequate help back to work.

Once people have become long-term unemployed employers are reluctant to hire them and they are rendered virtually unemployable. Therefore, when demand for labour expands the labour market acts as though the long-term unemployed do not exist and 'tightens' – thereby generating inflationary pressure – even when unemployment is very high. The build-up in long-term unemployment since the 1970s – when one in five jobless people had been without work for over a year compared with one in three at present – is therefore one reason why inflationary pressures emerge nowadays at much higher rates of unemployment.

Layard thus makes the case for more extensive use of active labour market policies to eliminate long-term unemployment which he considers to be a total waste of human resources. In a phrase that echoes Beveridge, Layard argues that the state should *"stop subsidising idleness and subsidise work instead"*. Active labour market measures include improved employment services (to improve the amount and quality of job search undertaken by unemployed people) and training for the jobless. But in his paper Layard stresses in particular the use of temporary employment as a means of preventing people becoming long-term unemployed. After a person has been unemployed for a year, Layard argues, the state should immediately take responsibility for providing that person with a temporary job as an alternative to providing benefit.

Layard counters the common objection that providing jobs for unemployed people in this way will merely take jobs away from other people. He posits that a period of work experience will mean that a long-term unemployed person becomes more employable than would be the case if he or she remained unemployed. Making the long-term unemployed more employable in this way means that employers have a larger pool of workers to choose from when seeking to fill vacancies. This reduces pressure on wages and prices and enables demand to expand farther than it otherwise would without stoking up inflation. The result is a higher level of employment overall.

The essential thing to ensure is that the temporary jobs offered to long-term unemployed people really make them more employable which is why Layard is adamant that the jobs should be with regular employers. If the jobs are of a 'make work' kind people employed in them will be little better off than had they simply remained on the dole. Unfortunately, this has too often been the case with the succession of temporary jobs programmes operated in Britain over the years. It is perhaps not surprising therefore that such programmes have often been viewed as little more than a means of 'disguising' the unemployment figures.

The same basic argument underlies the proposal by Dennis Snower – set out in a background note for the conference – for a 'Benefit Transfer Programme'. Snower advocates converting the value of benefits paid to unemployed people into a subsidy paid to employers. The unemployed person recieves the normal rate for the job but the cost to the employer is reduced thereby encouraging more recruitment. Snower's proposal has been implemented in a watered down fashion as the government's pilot 'Workstart' programme.[18] The latter, however, is targeted at the very long-term unemployed whereas Snower, like Layard, argues that policy must aim to *prevent* people becoming long-term unemployed in the first place, otherwise it will prove more difficult – and more costly – to help them back to work.

During the conference Richard Layard made it clear that there were potential problems involved in creating real jobs rather than 'make work' jobs in this way – not least the possibility that employers might lay off existing workers in order to replace them with subsidised workers. Such problems were not insurmountable, however, if imaginative thought was devoted to them. Layard thus called upon employers and unions to form a working group alongside policy makers to consider all the relevant practical issues and also devise appropriate safeguards against abuse, etc.

One delegate, Ms Olivia Grant, Chief Executive of Tyneside Training and Enterprise Council, while agreeing with the broad thrust of Richard Layard's argument, questioned the wisdom of providing temporary jobs without training.

She argued that periods of subsidised employment should be combined with training for a National Vocational Qualification. Suitable upskilling in this way would help increase the chances that a person would keep or soon get a job once their subsidised job came to an end. Richard Layard agreed that training was important but still thought it preferable to keep employment and training programmes separate. Mixing the two had in the past often led to very low quality training that was not very cost effective – thus enabling the Treasury to block extra funding for training programmes for the long-term unemployed. It was therefore better, Layard contended, to encourage high quality training programmes offering a good rate of return alongside clearly cost effective employment programmes of the kind he advocated.

The public sector and 'social employment'
The Snower and Layard proposals are compelling and (if made to operate effectively) seem to convey the considerable advantage of curing a major social and economic problem at little or no cost to the taxpayer. Some, however, would argue the social case for providing more jobs for the unemployed even if this did involve some additional sacrifice on the part of taxpayers or wage earners.

Paul Ormerod *op.cit.*, for example, argues that an economy's average rate of unemployment over the long-term is ultimately determined by prevailing social values and institutions. Hence the vastly different unemployment records of countries which have experienced comparable rates of economic growth. For Ormerod, therefore, technical economics tell us little of value about how to secure full employment. Neither counter-cyclical policies nor supply side policies designed to raise the growth potential of an economy – worthwhile though these may be – are likely to eat into core unemployment. What matters instead is the degree to which a society is prepared to ensure that the fruits of growth are fairly distributed.

In his paper and at the conference Ormerod cited various 'models' that did or would produce a fairer distribution of work opportunities. Japan was an example of a society which has been willing to bear the cost (in terms of higher prices for consumer services) of a relatively inefficient private service sector providing jobs for low productivity people who in Britain and many other European Union countries would remain unemployed. Elsewhere, notably the non-EU western European countries, the same outcome has been achieved by way of the state acting as 'employer of last resort' (with the taxpayer bearing the cost). Ormerod suggests that voluntarily 'work-sharing' linked to income-sharing could perform a similar redistributive function and help Britain back to full employment. Citing the recent experience of *Volkswagen* he suggested that German society showed signs of moving in this direction. But – as with a Citizen's Income – the task of achieving the necessary shift in social values in Britain would be considerable and extend well beyond the realm of economics.

In his paper, *Full Employment: The Role of the Public Sector*, Chris Trinder illustrates that for much of the post-war period the public sector in Britain performed a similar sort of 'social safety valve' function in the labour market by preserving jobs at a time when private sector employers were shedding them. However, successive privatisations and the drive for public sector managers to emulate those in the private sector has in recent years undermined this role. Trinder considers it short-sighted for the public sector to 'downsize' during recessions because any savings the Exchequer makes on labour costs is offset by the cost of keeping people unemployed. The perversity of this is that the burden of unemployment – made worse by private sector job losses – drives up public borrowing with the result that the government has to look for further cost savings. One consequence has been the freeze on public sector pay bills which means that already low paid public employees are forced to choose between higher pay or the possibility of further job losses.

Trinder suggests that this approach ought to be re-evaluated, especially when one considers that while making public sector workers redundant from regular jobs, the government is having to finance temporary (and generally inferior) jobs for the long-term unemployed under programmes such as 'Community Action'. Trinder instead argues that there is considerable scope for increasing normal public sector employment to meet pressing social and economic need, providing this can be financed. The key, however, will be to ensure that such an approach operates in tandem with a broader full employment strategy designed to create jobs in the private sector as well. Notwithstanding the basic merit in the argument for what might be called 'social solidarity', if public sector employment is seen as no more than an instrument for 'mopping-up' unemployment caused by broader economic failure taxpayers may prove reluctant to finance it.

Kevin Coyne, a delegate from the TUC unemployed centres, placed considerable stress on the role of the public sector in addressing the social need for more employment. He linked the issue of more publicly funded job creation with the suggestions of Patricia Hewitt and Paul Ormerod for family friendly working and work sharing. Whilst not disagreeing with the latter policies he felt that these made most sense for better off people who would happily trade income for more leisure time. For disadvantaged people in run down areas the real need was for long-term full-time jobs offering a living wage. Mr Coyne believed that society would ultimately have to face up to the fact that massive public investment was required to create jobs of the type that people wanted and needed.

Macroeconomic issues

A re-reading of the 1944 White Paper and the work of Beveridge is above all important in one particular aspect: it reminds us of the significance of demand. It is common nowadays for macroeconomics to lurk only in the background of debate on employment policy, while discussion of macro-issues often ignores employment. Admittedly, supply side problems would seem to contribute more to unemployment in 1994 than was the case in 1944. But one should not be swept away by current fashion which suggests that 'full employability' – admirable though the aim might be – is a substitute for 'full employment'. The levers of demand must be made sensitive to supply side improvements. To cut through unemployment it is necessary to use the twin scissors of demand *and* supply side policies (both of which will interact). As the OECD *Jobs Study* remarks, employment policy will be better adjusted if there is a 'synergy' between macroeconomic and supply side policy.

Most people are in general agreement that a stable macroeconomic background is essential for steady sustained growth, enabling investment in capacity and skills. However, the nature of macroeconomic policy is also important. James Meade, for example, argues that macroeconomic policy is at present too wedded to simple monetary based inflation targets when what one really wants is a policy that controls inflation without incurring a major sacrifice of output and employment. He therefore suggests that government should once again attempt to control aggregate expenditure in the economy using both monetary and fiscal instruments.[19]

Meade's proposal seems highly sensible, especially when one realises the havoc wreaked on the underlying economy by prolonged bouts of recession. Such an approach would have helped avoid the present log-jam caused by the high level of public borrowing. This is considered a constraint on the government's room for maneouvre in terms of financial policy. Had a more far-sighted counter-cyclical policy been applied at the onset of recession it is probable that the Budget deficit – as well as unemployment – would be lower.

For example, the government could have financed house building or infra-structure investment programmes, employing redundant construction workers in the short-term and creating public assets for the future. A greater sense of the importance of the real economy of output and jobs should therefore be instilled into macroeconomic policy. This is true at domestic and international levels where – with economies increasingly integrated through trade – policy co-ordination is vital. It is especially true at European level where, despite the laudable aims of the Delors White Paper,[20] financial policy is still underlaid by a fairly crude form of Euro-monetarism.

Pay and productivity

Whatever the chosen mix of supply and demand side policies within a full employment strategy one issue remains outstanding – how to handle the possibility of a pay-price 'spiral' as demand expands. Beveridge and the authors of the 1944 White Paper were well aware of the potential difficulties that could be caused by what is sometimes referred to as the British 'pay problem'.[21] For much of the post-war period a succession of prices and incomes policies sought to overcome this problem. Unfortunately, formal incomes policies proved difficult to sustain and have fallen out of fashion since the 1970s.

Workers and trade unions are rightly perplexed when they hear it suggested that Britain has a 'pay problem', since on average real pay in Britain is low by international standards. It is necessary, however, to distinguish the issue of real pay from that of pay inflation. Real pay is relatively low in Britain because on average productivity is low. Over time, productivity rises enabling growth in real pay. The 'pay problem' arises simply because of a tendency for pay increases to grow at a faster rate than productivity. This is especially true when demand for labour is buoyant (and even more so when skill shortages are significant and the long-term unemployed are very numerous). When this occurs, the result is (unit) wage cost inflation and (usually) price inflation. Although the higher price inflation will tend to diminish the real value of a pay rise, those who are employed may nonetheless find themselves to be better off. But there will also be losers if the government responds to the inflation by depressing demand and allowing unemployment to rise.

A major reason why 'core' unemployment has risen in Britain since the 1970s is precisely because the government has resorted to unemployment as a means of keeping inflation in check. This is the worst kind of 'incomes policy'. A strategy for full employment would need to develop an alternative. Economy wide institutions are required that can help ensure that pay (i.e. 'earnings', not just wage settlements) rise on average no faster than the economy can afford. Sadly, as William Brown shows in his paper, *Bargaining for Full Employment: Social Partnership and Wage Determination*, economic and industrial relations institutions have, since the late 1970s, become less conducive to keeping pay in step with productivity. Pay bargaining has become more fragmented in both the private and public sectors, while government has been generally hostile to national forums – such as NEDO – where the issues surrounding pay and productivity could be discussed by the 'social partners'.

Brown argues that building a full employment policy will require a renaissance of collective institutions – albeit not a simple resurrection of old ones – for employers, for employees and for bargaining between them. Social partnership will be an essential requirement. One might add that it will also be necessary to ensure that any new institutions are seen as a means of fostering prospects for long-run improvements in real pay as well as bringing about an accommodation between short-run movements in pay and productivity. Otherwise there is a danger that attention will focus too narrowly on pay and ignore the broader problem of poor economic performance.

Barry Lewis, a delegate from USDAW, asked the conference panellists for their views on the role of incomes policy as part of any strategy for full employment – and whether any such policy should cover profits and prices as well as wages. The panellists failed to address the latter point. But Richard Layard emphasised that in most countries where core unemployment was relatively low, constant and painstaking effort on the part of the social partners was required to prevent an inflationary average pay rise.

For Layard the issue was not one of a formal state imposed incomes policy but rather that of encouraging ways for the social partners to work together to achieve a more desirable 'trade-off' between inflation and unemployment. Overseas experience, Layard suggested, indicated that solidarity between employers – involving the co-ordination of pay bargaining – would be a key condition. Paul Ormerod broadly agreed. Ormerod argued, however, that the fact that countries where pay bargaining is co-ordinated also manage to achieve lower unemployment rates simply reflects broader social values. The central issue, according to Ormerod, is not pay co-ordination *per se* but the fact that some societies appear more willing and able than others to organise their economic and social institutions within a co-operative framework.

Setting targets?

Having considered some of the issues that would surround the development of a strategy for full employment it is worth concluding by giving some thought to the sort of time scale involved for attaining the goal. The three per cent unemployment rate envisaged by Beveridge remains a worthwhile target but will, in a free market economy, require painstaking effort over many years to achieve. It is twenty years since full employment was last attained; few can be confident that full employment could be re-attained in less than ten to fifteen. Moreover, the future is uncertain – even the best of policies must accept the possibility of as yet unforseen shocks or strains on the system. What is vitally important, however, is that the necessary measures are set in train immediately to move us toward much fuller employment.

The uncertainty surrounding the future makes it difficult to guarantee that any precise target set for full employment could be met. Targets – such as the aim set out in the Delors White Paper to cut European Union unemployment in half by 2000 – are nonetheless useful because they offer a benchmark against which progress can be measured.

Setting targets will require detailed knowledge of the magnitude of the task before us, so good unemployment statistics are needed. The use and publication of jobless figures will have to be reformed. The EPI has advocated introducing the system operated by the US Bureau of Labor Statistics. This involves publishing a range of unemployment rates derived from the Labour Force Survey. The range would include not only the standard ILO measure of people unemployed and actively seeking jobs but also a measure of people who want a job but have given up searching for one.[22]

Detailed work needs to be done to calculate a precise job creation target for full employment. A rough calculation of the numbers currently in the labour market and those who would enter in more buoyant times suggests a target figure of at least four million net new jobs (other things being equal). This is a tall order, although one must not forget that when demand expanded rapidly during the 'Lawson Boom' of the late 1980s jobs were created at a remarkable rate. The difficult problem is not so much creating jobs as sustaining them.

Looking forward to full employment

Reducing unemployment by the required amount will certainly involve some sacrifices. In particular, society will have to face up to the fact that investment – private and public, in industrial capacity and in people – must take priority over consumption for a period of years. Economic renewal and the need to offer every citizen a full stake in society demands this. Social justice also demands that the burden of adjustment from a largely acquisitive society to one that seeks to further the common good must fall primarily upon those most able to bear it.

These truths may be difficult for politicians to convey to the electorate in a modern free society even though success would ultimately pay a handsome economic and social dividend. It will therefore be necessary to spell out that the dividend would accrue to all, not just those currently at risk of social exclusion. As several delegates pointed out at the conference, a successful move toward full employment will almost certainly have to be based upon a new 'social settlement'.

Fortunately, for the first time in years, the relatively prosperous may be more receptive to the message of full employment now that the 'culture of contentment' has given way to a 'culture of anxiety'. Many in the prosperous 'middle-third' of society, who in the 1980s thought themselves immune from unemployment and job insecurity, have faced a rude awakening in the 1990s. Having taken for granted the ability to cover long-term mortgage commitments and forge a reasonable life-style, many are uncertain about the future. A practical strategy for tackling unemployment and adapting to change in the labour market would thus garner support from all sections of society. It is time to develop such a strategy. It is time for Britain to look forward to full employment.

References (other than background papers shown at Annex B)

[1] Beveridge, W. H. (1994). *Full Employment in a Free Society*. Unwin Brothers Ltd.

[2] HM Government (1994). *Employment Policy*, Cmnd 6527. HMSO.

[3] Meade, J. E. (1994). *Full Employment Without Inflation*. Employment Policy Institute and Social Market Foundation.

[4] Philpott, J. (1994). "The Incidence and Cost of Unemployment". In Glyn, A. and Miliband, D. (Eds) *Paying for Inequality: the Economic Cost of Social Injustice*. Rivers Oram Press/Institute for Public Policy Research.

[5] Schmitt, J. and Wadsworth, J. (1994). "The Rise in Economic Inactivity". In Glyn, A. and Miliband, D. *op. cit.*

[6] Wood, A. (1994). *North–South Trade, Employment and Inequality*. Oxford, Clarendon Press.

[7] Organisation for Economic Co-operation and Development (1994). *OECD Jobs Study: Facts, Analysis, Strategies*. OECD, Paris.

[8] Goodhart, D. (1994). *The Reshaping of the German Social Market*. Institute for Public Policy Research.

[9] Balls, E. and Gregg, P. (1993). *Work and Welfare*. Institute for Public Policy Research.

[10] Clarke, K. (1994). "The Changing World of Work in the 1990s". Fifteenth Annual Mais Lecture, City University Business School.

[11] See also Mayhew, K. (1994). "Labour Market Woes". *New Economy*, volume 1, issue 2. Institute for Public Policy Research.

[12] Balls, E. (1994). "Looking Beyond the Flexibility Rhetoric". *The Guardian*, 6th June 1994.

[13] Brown, C. (1990). "Racial Inequality in the British Labour Market". Employment Policy Institute *Economic Report*, June.

[14] HM Government (1994). "Competitiveness: Helping Business to Win", Cmnd 2563. HMSO.

[15] House of Commons, Select Committee on Trade and Industry (1994). "Competitiveness of UK Manufacturing Industry". Second Report, Session 1993–94. HMSO.

[16] Buxton, T., Chapman, P. and Temple, P. (1994). *Britain's Economic Performance*. Routledge.

[17] McLaughlin, E. (1994). *Flexibility in Work and Benefits*. Institute for Public Policy Research.

[18] Employment Policy Institute (1993). "Making Workstart Work". EPI *Economic Report*, volume 7, number 8, April.

[19] Meade (1994). *op. cit.*

[20] European Commission (1993). "Growth, Competitiveness and Employment". White Paper.

[21] Bayliss, F. J. (1993). *Does Britain Still Have a Pay Problem?*. Employment Policy Institute.

[22] Employment Policy Institute (1994). "Measure for Measure". *Economic Report*, volume 8, number 2, March.

CHAPTER 6

The future agenda

The TUC and EPI conference made a significant contribution to changing the shape of the economic and political debate in the second half of the 1990s. For the first time in nearly 15 years, full employment is being discussed as a serious policy option.

All three political parties have agreed on the concept, albeit with varying degrees of commitment. A wide range of interests outside the political parties believe full employment is both desirable and can, in the medium term, be achieved.

This debate is not confined to Britain. There are 35 million out of work in the industrial world, many of them in Europe. There is a new urgency in the Organisation for Economic Co-operation and Development to develop an effective response. The OECD *Jobs Study* and 1994 *Employment Outlook* are an important contribution to the policy debate. The European Commission's White Paper on Growth, Competitiveness and Employment sets out a potential framework for taking Europe forward.

The most important question is, of course, what to do next. Keeping full employment at the centre of the economic and political debates is now a central task for the TUC, the Employment Policy Institute, and others who share this objective.

One important task is to build on the ideas set out in the conference papers and the speeches and contributions made at the conference itself. This will mean developing the existing links the TUC and trade unions have with institutions and individuals, pressure groups, and campaign organisations, as well as building new ones. The aim must be to build constructive and credible policies, to move beyond vague and general slogans to practical proposals for action.

The range of policy issues which could be covered is vast (see the TUC's six principles for full employment as shown at Annex D). But some of our first priorities will be looking at help for the long-term unemployed; the future of benefits and the welfare state; low pay and casualisation of work; and the macroeconomic framework.

As one immediate example of the approach, the TUC is linking with a range of organisations to look at how changes in the benefit system can genuinely help people back to work – in contrast to the coercive approach underpinning the new Jobseekers' Allowance.

The 1994 Unified Budget in November provides the next major opportunity to enter into the public debate with positive proposals on job generation, including the role of job creation subsidies, the tax and benefit system, and public investment programmes. Our aim is to develop proposals which could make the 1994 Budget, a Budget for Full Employment.

The effective development of policy will require a wide ranging public debate, reflecting the outward focus of the July 5 conference. The TUC will be holding a series of regional conferences in 1994 and 1995 to bring together trade unionists, the unemployed, and other organisations – business, academic, voluntary sector, the churches, to discuss ideas on job creation and helping the unemployed.

Developing an effective agenda for action will be a challenge, but it is one which must be faced. Even a sustained economic recovery will leave around two million people unemployed by internationally agreed (i.e. ILO) criteria, and many others outside the labour market who would nonetheless like to work.

There are also two further challenges. One is help for the long-term unemployed. When unemployment fell in 1993 the fall was confined to those out of work for less than 12 months. Long-term unemployment, in contrast, went up on the ILO definition during 1993, and has only recently begun to fall very slightly.

The other is to ensure that those who historically have suffered from high unemployment – young people, black workers, people with disabilities – get a fair share of jobs and training opportunities in the future. And there is an equally urgent need to address the problems of inequalities in access to quality jobs and education and training opportunities for women. These must be an integral part of our approach to full employment.

Contributing to this debate, moving the agenda on, campaigning for positive change – these are all urgent priorities for the trade union movement and the EPI, both in Britain and at the international level.

Looking forward to full employment

Congress House, July 5th, 1994

09.15   **Registration/Coffee**

09.40   **Welcoming address:** Rodney Bickerstaffe
(Member of the TUC General Council)

09.50   **Profiles of unemployment today:**
Five individually delivered case histories

10.10   **"Full employment – is it still possible?":** Andrew Britton,
Director of the National Institute for Economic and Social Research

10.35   **Coffee**

10.45   Richard Lambert, Editor, Financial Times, introduced –
**"The challenge: working together towards full employment . . .
towards a partnership":** Keynote address by John Monks,
General Secretary, TUC

11.05   **Responses to the challenge:**
Employers: Howard Davies, Director General CBI
Government: The Right Hon. David Hunt, MBE, MP,
Secretary of State for Employment

11.45   **Question Time:** Chaired by Francine Stock, BBC TV:
panel composed of Howard Davies, David Hunt and John Monks

12.15   **Action Profiles:** Four individually delivered case histories of
employment-creating experiences and successes

12.35   **Lunch**

13.35   Rodney Bickerstaffe introduced –
Labour's View: John Prescott, MP,
Front Bench Spokesperson on Employment

13.55   **Debate: "Is full employment possible? If so, how?"**
Chaired by Francine Stock. *The panel –*
Herman Ouseley, Chair, Commission for Racial Equality;
Kamlesh Bahl, Chair, Equal Opportunities Commission;
Alex Carlile, QC, MP, Liberal Democrats;

Patricia Hewitt, Deputy Director-General, IPPR;
Professor Paul Ormerod, Economist, Chair, Full Employment UK;
Professor Richard Layard, LSE
After the panellists' opening contributions, the debate was
thrown open to the floor

15.30 **"Where do we go from here?":**
Reply from John Philpott, Director, Employment Policy Institute
and Bill Callaghan, Head of Economic and Social Affairs
Department, TUC

15.50 **End**

Attendance list

Ms Ann Abraham	*NACAB*
Peter Agar	*CBI*
Ms Irene Aldridge	*St Ivel*
Alex Alexandrou	*CMA*
Adrian Alsop	*ESRC*
Ray Andrews	*AEEU*
Sam Apter	*MSF*
Martin Arnott	*CITB*
Peter Ashby	*Full Employment UK*
Dr C. B. Ayisa	*Leicester City Council*
M. J. Backs	*NUIW*
Ruth Badger	*Board for Social Responsibility*
Kamlesh Bahl	*Equal Opportunities Commission*
Edward Balls	*Gordon Brown's Office*
Nicholas Baring	*Baring Foundation*
John Bartell	*POA*
Michael A. Barrett	*NLBD*
Kevin Barron, MP	*House of Commons*
Fred Bayliss	*EPI*
Les Bayliss	*ICOM/TU Working Party*
Johnathon Baume	*FDA*
Adam Baxter	*Japanese Embassy*
Geoff Beacon	*Education Resources*
Johnathon Beard	*St John's College, Cambridge*
J. B. Beard	*Cambridge University*
Eric Bellenie	*Over Fifties Association*
Hillary Benn	*MSF*
Mark Bennister	*House of Commons*
Dr F. M. Bhatti	*Council of Mosques*
Rodney Bickerstaffe	*UNISON*
Syd Bill	*Staffs TEC*
Giles Bloomer	*Rotherham TEC*
Roger Bolton	*BECTU*
Peter Bottomley, MP	*House of Commons*
Helen Bradburn	*Shelter*
Moira Brady	*SFMTA*
Peter Brannen	*ILO*

Ms N. Bray	
Bill Brett	*IPMS*
Andrew Britton	*NIESR*
Peter Brook	*Liberal Democrats*
Clive Brooke	*IRSF*
G. Bromlow	
Andrew Brown	*Worcester Welfare Rights*
Bill Brown	*Unions 94*
Malcolm Brown	*William Temple Foundation*
Prof William Brown	*Cambridge University*
George Brumwell	*UCATT*
Dr Chris Burchall	*University of Cambridge*
Dorothy Burnett	*UCW*
Giles Burrows	*MSF*
Jose Calas	*Spanish Embassy*
Barry Caldy	*North London TEC*
R. I. Cambridge	*BTEC*
Doreen Cameron	*NATFHE*
Ken Cameron	*FBU*
Sandra Campbell	*London Borough of Bromley*
David Campbell-Bannerman	*BOW Group*
Alex Carlile, QC, MP	*House of Commons*
Mike Carney	*NASUWT*
Bernard Carter	*Employment Department*
Sir John Cassels	*National Commission on Education*
Ian F. Catty	*Assoc Liberal Democrats*
Mr Chalphin	*IOD*
Mark Champion	*NZTV – CRT*
Maurice Chittock	*Unemployed*
Alan Churchard	*CPSA*
Richard Clements	*Citizens Income*
Mr A. W. Clowes	*CATU*
Ann Clwyd, MP	*House of Commons*
John Creaby, MBE	*GMB*
Austin Crick	*Student*
Peter Coldrick	*ETUC*
Peter Cole	*NUSUWT*
S. Collins	*Clydebank UCRC*
Prof T. Congdon	*Lombard Street Research*

Angela Conlin	
Mick Connolly	*SERTUC*
Bill Connor	*USDAW*
Paul Convery	*Unemployment Unit*
James Cornford	*IPPR*
R. Cornell	*AEEU*
Kevin Coyne	*MTUCWRC*
Simon Crine	*Fabian Society*
Robin Daley	*FDA*
Mark Darke	*Leeds Metropolitan University*
Howard Davies	*CBI*
Trudi Brake Danby	*Nuffield Foundation*
Ms Lucy Daniels	*Parents at Work*
Stan Davison	*Unions 94*
Nigel DeGruchy	*NASUWT*
John Dewsbury	*Employment Department*
Mrs S. Diplock	*Fawcett Society*
Janice Dickson	
Keith Dolling	*Sandwell TEC*
Frank Doran	*TUCC*
Scott Douglas	*Landrover*
Tony Dubbins	*GPMU*
Dave Ellis	*Low Pay Unit*
John Ellis	*CCSU*
Dr Walter Eltis	*DTI*
David Evans	*POA*
John Evans	*TUAC-OECD*
Nigel Evans, MP	*House of Commons*
M. J. Fellowes	*Hotel & Catering Training Co*
Frank Field, MP	*House of Commons*
Tony Finn	*GMB TEC Director*
David Foden	*ETUI*
John Flavin	*UCATT*
Kevin Flynn	*TUC UWCs*
Maureen Fountaine	
John Foster	*NUJ*
Chris Freeman	*University of Sussex*

Bob Fryer	*Northern College*
Carol Fussey	*Humberside TEC*
Paul Gates	*KFAT*
Duncan Gallie	*Nuffield College*
Eddie George	*Bank of England*
Anne Gibson	*MSF*
Jim Gillespie	*NUIW*
D. O. Gladwyn	*TUCC*
Robbie Gilbert	*CBI*
John Gracie	*Qualitec Ltd*
Mike Graham	*South West TUC*
Olivia Grant	*Tyneside TEC*
David Grayson	*Business in the Community*
Dr C. A. Greenhalgh	*St Peter's College, Oxford*
Dennis Gregory	*Ruskin College*
Dr Mary Gregory	*University of Oxford*
Frank Griffiths	*Lib Dem Trade Unionists*
Owen Gunn	
Ann Hacker	*West London TEC*
Liam Halligan	*Oxford University*
Carl Hadley	*West Wales TEC*
Colin Hampton	*Derbyshire UWC*
J. F. Hansford	*Basildon TUC*
Mike Hanson	*South Thames TEC*
Peter Harvey	*EPI*
Ms Pat Hawkes	*NUT*
Rose Hayward	*Royal National Theatre*
Mr Heald, MP	*House of Commons*
Simon Hebditch	*Nat Council for Voluntary Organisations*
Kim Hendry	*BIFU*
Ms D. Hergest	*Electricity Association*
Patricia Hewitt	*IPPR*
Bernadette Hillon	*USDAW*
John Hills	*Joseph Rowntree Foundation*
Graham Hitchen	*British Youth Council*
David Higginbottom	*URTU*
John Hills	*London School of Economics*
Martin Hughes	*AUT*
Chris Humphries	*TEC National Council*

Rt Hon David Hunt, MBE, MP	*House of Commons*
Mrs Lynne Hope	*Staffordshire TEC*
Bob Howard	*NTUC*
Marylin Howard	*Disability Alliance*
Brenda Hudson	*UNISON*
Paul Jagger	*Yorks & Humberside TUC*
Terry Jarman	*POA*
David Jenkins	*Wales TUC*
Alan Jinkinson	*UNISON*
Barry Johnson	*TUC Unemployed Centres*
Carolyn Jones	*Institute of Employment Rights*
Roger Jones	*Gwent TEC*
Kathleen Jones	*NAP*
M. A. Judge	*Peugeot Talbot*
Bishop John Jukes	*Board of Social Responsibility*
Carol Kay	*University of Warwick*
Phil Kemball	*IPMS*
Staffan Kellerborg	*Swedish Embassy*
Charlotte Kearns	*FDA*
Judith Kidd	*APEX Trust*
Rev Ermal Kirby	*Council of Churches for Britain & Ireland*
Mike Kirby	*Graphical Employment & Training Group*
Colin Knott	*NULMW*
Richard Lambert	*Editor, Financial Times*
Prof Richard Layard	*LSE*
Margaret Langley	*MSF*
Mark Layton	*IDS*
Clive W. Leach	*Leeds TEC*
Thomas Letang	*DCSA – CRT*
B. Lewis	*USDAW*
Maurice Littlewood	*Trustee EPI*
Richard Lloyd	*Shelter*
Tony Lloyd	*MP*
Graham Lord	*CAPITB Trust*
Julia Lourie	*House of Commons Library*
Ida Love	*UNISON*
John Lovelady	*CMA*

P. M. Luck	*MSF, Glos TEC*
Roger Lyons	*MSF*
W. McCarady	*NLBD*
Lord McCarthy	*Nuffield College*
John Macinnes	*University of Glasgow*
Sir Donald MacDougal	
C. MacKenzie	*AEEU*
Hector MacKenzie	*UNISON*
Ruth MacKenzie	*Nottingham Playhouse*
Tom McNally	*Democratic Left*
Richard McManus	
Rupert McNeil	*CBI*
J. J. Madden	*NALHM*
Denise Maguire	
Malcolm Maguire	*Centre for Labour Market Studies*
Jane Mann	*Women in Management*
John Mannell	*Devon & Cornwall TEC*
Dianne Marrin	*NCCUC*
B. J. Marshall	*Doncaster Council*
Dr Connie Martin	*Anglo-German Foundation*
David Martin	*IRS*
Diana Martin	*TUC UWC*
Hugh J. Martin	*GMB*
William Mather	*EPI*
Leslie Mawdsley	*Unemployed Centres*
Dr Ken Mayhew	*Pembroke College, Oxford*
Pamela Meadows	*PSI*
Monty Meth	*Carnegie Third Age*
Maria Middleton	*Wakefield Unemployed Centre*
Leif Mills	*BIFU*
Prof Lewis Minkin	*Northern College*
Bev Minter	*NUMAST*
Joseph Montgomery	*London Borough of Lewisham*
Andrew Morgan	*Democratic Left Law Group*
Elwyn Morgan	*GMB*
Mr M. Morgan	*Northern Foods Ltd*
Dominic Morris	*Policy Unit*
Peter Morris	*UNISON*
T. Morris	*UNISON*
Dr Geoff Mulgan	*DEMOS*

Sir Michael Neubert, MP	*House of Commons*
Bob Norris	*Assistant Secretary, NUJ*
Larry Nugent	*Glasgow Coalition of Disabled People*
David R. Nurse	*MSF – Oxford Health Branch*
Richard O'Brien	*EPI*
Prof Paul Ormerod	*Full Employment UK*
Herman Ouseley	*Commission for Racial Equality*
Tim Page	*House of Commons*
Mr H. Y. Pampel	*German Embassy*
Bharti Patel	*Low Pay Unit*
Ms S. Peacock	*Engineering Training Authority*
Ken Perry	*NUIW*
John Philpott	*EPI*
Prof David Piachaud	*LSE*
Frances Pickering	*FDA*
Melanie Pine	*Irish Embassy*
Malcolm Pitt	*Pontifical Council for Justice & Peace*
John Prescott, MP	*House of Commons*
Jocelyn Prudence	*Chartered Society of Physiotherapists*
Sid Platt	*Chair, West Midlands TUC*
Chris Pond	*Low Pay Unit*
Carol Popplewell	*CPSA*
Len Powell	*ISTC*
Patience Purdy	*National Council of Women GB*
Niu Qiang	*Chinese Embassy*
Rosemary Radcliffe	*Coopers & Lybrand*
Peter Rainbird	*Essex TEC*
Norman Record	
W. B. Reddaway	*Cambridge University*
Simon Rix	*University of London*
Dr James Robertson	*Employment Department*
Nick Robinson	*BBC*
Peter Robinson	*Centre for Economic Performance*
Cllr Jerry Rodhouse	*Warwickshire County Council*
Brian Rogers	
Tony Ronse	*CPSA*
Maureen Rooney	*AEEU*

John Rowland	
Jill Rubery	*UMIST*
Brendan Rutter	*GPMU*
Tanveer Salam	*Unemployed*
Arthur Sanderson	*Cumbria TEC*
Arthur Scott	*MSF*
Ronnie Scott	*FBU*
Jan Sec	*Polish Embassy*
Ron Seddon	*IRSF*
Baroness Seear	*House of Lords*
Dr Natuhlai Shah	
John Sheldon	*NUCPS*
Tom Sheard	*Barnsley TUC Training Ltd*
Jon Shields	*Bank of England*
Romy Shovelton	*WIKIMA*
Geeta Shrestha	*Sunderland TUC UWC*
Tom Sibley	*Institute of Employment Rights*
Ruth Silver	*Lewisham College*
Jim Skinner	*European Observatory*
Sue Slipman	*NCOPF*
John Grieve-Smith	*Robinson College, Cambridge*
M. Soave	*GPMU Kent*
Yvonne Spence	*Windsor Fellowship*
Bill Spiers	*Scottish TUC*
Jenny Spouge	*Luton Industrial College*
Bryan Stevens	*Involvement & Participation Organisation*
Mike Stewart	*NACRO*
Francine Stock	*BBC TV*
Catherine N. Stratton	*Business in the Community*
Graham Stone	*NCCUC*
Peter Stokoe	*EPI*
Barbara Switzer	*MFS*
R. H. M. Symons	*Dorset TEC*
Brian Robert Tagg	*ASLEF*
R. G. Taylor, CBE	*ABCC*
Michael Taylor	*IOD*
Nina Temple	*Unions 94*
Priti Thanki	*EPI*
Jenny Thurston	*IPMS*

D. W. Todd	*AEEU*
Warren Town	*Society of Radiographers*
Chris Trinder	*Public Finance Foundation*
David Triesman	*AUT*
George Tsogas	*Buckinghamshire College*
Derek Turner	*SPOA*
Peter Verheyen	*Netherlands Embassy*
Philip Walker	*CAADE*
Caroline Walsh	*Low Pay Unit*
Margaret Wallis	*Careers Advisory Service – Warwick*
Mike Ward	*NCCUC*
Raymond Ward	*NULMW*
Mr John Warnock	*American Embassy*
Sir Douglas Wass	*NOMURA International*
Tony Webb	*CBI*
Katrina Webster	*Age Concern*
Peter Wetzel	*Barnsley & Doncaster TEC*
Paul Whitehouse	*Sussex Police*
Neil Whycherley	*NCCUC*
Tony Wilkinson	*North Notts TEC*
David Wilson	*NUJ*
Tony Wilson	*AUT*
Christine Wood	*TUC Midlands Region*
Phil Woolas	*GMB Direct*
Richard Young	*EBEA*
Tony Young	*NCU*
L. Zylberberg	*French Embassy*

Note: Every effort has been made to ensure the above list is an accurate record. However, the list may still contain some errors and should be used with this caution in mind.

TUC–EPI Conference Papers

Looking Forward to Full Employment: An Overview (John Philpott, Director, Employment Policy Institute)

Full Employment in a Market Economy (Andrew Britton, Director, National Institute for Economic and Social Research)

A Price Worth Paying? (David Piachaud, London School of Economics)

What Do Women Want from Full Employment? (Jill Rubery, Manchester School of Management, UMIST)

Full Employment for Men and Women (Patricia Hewitt, Deputy Director, Institute for Public Policy Research)

Why Manufacturing Still Matters (Christine Greenhalgh and Mary Gregory, University of Oxford)

Technical Change and Unemployment (Chris Freeman, University of Sussex and University of Limburg)

Does Globalisation Threaten Low Skill Western Workers? (Richard Freeman, Harvard University)

Can Economics Solve the Problem of Unemployment? (Paul Ormerod, University of Manchester, POE Ltd and Chair, Full Employment UK)

Building Full Employment Without Low Pay (Chris Pond, Low Pay Unit)

Regulation v Deregulation: Which Way for Europe's Labour Market? (David Marsden, London School of Economics)

Preventing Long-Term Unemployment in Europe (Richard Layard, London School of Economics)

Full Employment: the Role of the Public Sector (Chris Trinder, Director, Public Finance Foundation)

Bargaining for Full Employment: Social Partnership and Wage Determination (William Brown, University of Cambridge)

Also available at the conference but not for wider publication:

UK Training Policy: Assumptions and Reality (Ewart Keep and Ken Mayhew, University of Oxford)

Converting Unemployment Benefits into Employment Subsidies (Dennis Snower, Birkbeck College)

ANNEX C

Four action profiles

1. Mr PAUL GATES, Knitwear and Apparel Trade Union. TUC Nominated Director, Bury and Bolton Training and Enterprise Council

This profile gives an insight into what happened when a relatively small company in the Bolton area, Halbro Sportswear, which was facing business difficulties, approached Bury and Bolton TEC for support under the Business Growth Training (BGT) Option 3 programme.

The company – founded in 1911 – had been producing one specialist product, rugby union jerseys, for a niche market of rugby clubs and high street sports shops. Business was stagnating and indeed even traditional orders were being lost. Management was therefore faced with one of two decisions – to backtrack or take a positive decision to go for expansion and growth.

The company sought the help of the TEC's Business Advice Team when it made the positive decision to go for growth. The TEC offered specialist assistance. In financial terms this took the form of matched funding under BGT. Practical assistance was also provided. This took the form of training and help in improving management systems and product quality so that the company could widen its market.

The action that was taken focused first of all on the decision to expand the business beyond the domestic rugby union market. The company began selling in France, Japan and the US. It also began to produce fashion replica jerseys for the leisure wear market and diversified into soccer kits.

The company immediately benefited from the changes it had made with regard to training. Every employee – the majority of whom are women – was given an individual training plan with an emphasis on multi-skilling. The training programme was instituted with the co-operation of the workforce and unions. An internal training school was set up for new employees to replace the traditional "sitting by Nellie" approach to training.

The changes in manufacturing methods reduced work in progress and unit costs, while a quality initiative programme had the effect of reducing reject levels by 10 per cent. For employees, greater job satisfaction has been highlighted in two ways. Labour turnover was reduced by 10 per cent, while absenteeism which was running above 15 per cent dropped below 10 per cent. Short-time working – so often a problem in the clothing industry – is now virtually unknown in the company and the number of employees has increased from 127 in 1991 to 160 today.

This is an example of what can be achieved if a company takes positive action to improve its situation. The company is now taking advantage of other support from the TEC to help it achieve Investor in People status and World Class Company status. Above all this example shows what can be achieved in co-operation with the workforce in building a business and going forward to success.

2. Mr TOM SHEARD, General Manager, Barnsley TUC Training Ltd

Barnsley TUC Training Ltd employs 20 people to provide quality training to adults, both employed and unemployed. The directors are local trade unionists which gives the company a rather different perspective on education and training.

This profile demonstrates the role played by the company in economic regeneration in Barnsley. Barnsley has significant economic problems. The unemployment rate currently stands at 14.7 per cent. Traditional industries are in decline. Over the past 10 years more than 20,000 jobs have been lost from mining alone. The borough has one of the lowest take-up rates of education and training in Britain and Barnsley school-leavers are amongst the lowest achievers in terms of academic qualifications. In the past the area has also been unattractive to potential investors and this has led to a sense of despair, particularly amongst the unemployed.

In facing up to these problems, Barnsley trade unions decided they must make a positive contribution by forming partnerships with other agencies. This enabled the unions to influence the regeneration process, to improve the chances of making progress, and to promote trade union values to a wider audience.

Barnsley needs investment – both in capital and in people. Capital investment has been led by the public sector. The government and local authorities have undertaken significant programmes and partnerships to improve the infrastructure and attract private sector development. Investment in people has been led by a partnership between the local Barnsley and Doncaster TEC, local authorities and local training providers. The aim has been to create a competitive and dynamic workforce with skills to meet the requirements of both new and existing employers.

The trade unions have assisted this process in a practical way, especially with regard to improving the local skills base. Trade unions can encourage employers to introduce training programmes, encourage individuals to take up training, monitor the quality of training, promote equal opportunities, and as Barnsley TUC Training has done become a direct provider of training.

In terms of results the trade union movement has made a significant impact on the drive toward economic regeneration in Barnsley. The trade union movement is a partner in the Barnsley Economic Regeneration Forum, the mechanism for bidding for the government's new Single Regeneration Budget.

As a direct training provider, Barnsley TUC Training has in 1993–94 trained 140 people and of these 113 have obtained National Vocational Qualifications, with 44 going into employment or further or higher education. In addition, Barnsley TUC Training and the Yorkshire and Humberside Regional TUC have formed a partnership with Barnsley and Doncaster TEC to promote education and training amongst trade union members and encourage trade union involvement in training.

From a national perspective these achievements may seem quite small. But we believe they are positive initiatives that can and should be developed elsewhere. The key message is that of partnership toward a common aim. However, if partnership is to succeed it is important that all partners are allowed to contribute so that mutual trust and understanding can develop. As the old Chinese proverb says: Tell me and I will forget. Show me and I will remember. Involve me and I will understand.

3. Mr SCOTT DOUGLAS, Personnel Operations Director, LandRover

This profile illustrates the success that LandRover has had at creating employment over the past 12–14 months.

LandRover is part of the Rover Group. In addition to LandRover manufacture – including the Defender and Discovery range – at Solihull, the Group also produces the 500 and 600 series at Cowley and small and medium-sized cars at Longbridge. The history had been one of industrial conflict and a poor quality unattractive product range which was largely uncompetitive. In the late 1980s therefore, the company under Sir Graham Day and George Simpson, decided on a number of key strategies:

(1)   To break out of the UK market and grow in Europe and the rest of the world;

(2)   To break-even and become more competitive;

(3)   To move upmarket and move out of volume manufacturing;

(4)   To become Number One in customer quality.

This led to a vision statement – Extraordinary Customer Satisfaction – and the Group has spent years ensuring that employees identify with the statement.

The statement has resulted in a Total Quality Approach involving a fundamental change in the culture of the business. In particular there was a shift away from a largely autocratic 'tell, instruct' approach to management, to one in which employees are continually involved. This new approach has gained the support of the trade unions. Although there are still problems on a day to day basis there is far less confrontation than in the past.

A milestone was the agreement with the trade unions signed in April 1992 – "Rover Tomorrow, The New Deal". This established a framework for working together and managing the business. The Deal was about creating an environment of Single Status. Clocking was abandoned, lay-offs were ruled out, and health checks were provided for all employees. In addition, a job security phrase (i.e. everybody who wants to work with Rover can continue to do so) was instituted and stress was placed on the need for continuing improvement through learning and development.

The agreement is not a traditional 'if you give us this we will give you some money' deal. It was hammered out in the middle of a two year pay deal period. Its main objectives were and are to encourage every individual to contribute toward improving the business, to provide long-term job security, promote individual development and increase flexibility so that the Group becomes more competitive.

The benefits to the business have been clear. There has been unprecedented demand for products amid a perception of improved product quality. In 1992, 60,000 vehicles were being produced each year; this has increased to 100,000 at present. 12,000 new jobs have been created and there are more to come. It has also been possible to move people around the group. Where, for example, there has been a slump in demand for cars, employees have been moved to other product areas. This has enabled the company to fulfil its commitment to long-term job security.

This success has been based upon a partnership and sense of common purpose to take the company and its workers forward to success.

4. Mrs GEETA SHRESTHA,
Sunderland TUC Unemployed Centre

This profile highlights the difficulties faced by women from ethnic minority backgrounds and then outlines the efforts to help them overcome the language and cultural barriers that prevent them from obtaining skills.

Sunderland has only a relatively small Asian population. Few in the population are educated or have good jobs. Few mix freely with local people.

In 1981 Geeta – a teacher from Nepal – was given responsibility for running the local multi-cultural women's skill project. This involved bringing Asian women to a small craft centre. Although there was a creche the centre had few other facilities. Geeta had to use her own knitting machine for teaching purposes. Moreover the only pattern books and magazines were in English and Geeta normally had to teach the women in their own language.

The project has succeeded in providing women with skills and access to employment opportunities. But it is also important that the women have been able to venture outside their homes. In this respect Geeta has had to establish personal contacts in the Asian community demonstrating to husbands the advantages of providing skills to their wives.

117

The TUC's six principles for full employment

★ **Working Together:** government, employers and trade unions to accept the 1944 White Paper challenge, and take responsibility for the number of people in work.

★ **Working with the Unemployed:** development of quality work and training programmes to help the long-term unemployed, and through Unemployed Workers' Centres and other agencies, offer practical help, advice and support.

★ **Working for Equality:** improving women's position in the labour market, ensuring fair access to jobs for young people, black people and disabled people.

★ **Working for Security with Flexibility:** giving people the confidence for a lifetime of change by promoting quality and secure employment, based on investment in quality training and education.

★ **Working for Competitiveness:** building a strong internationally traded sector through active industrial policy, investment in transport and electronic information networks, support for research and development, and developing the regions.

★ **Working with Europe:** rebuilding co-operation and trust in Europe for a co-operative growth strategy in the 1990s.